PRAISE FOR DR. RUTH

"Her energy level is higher than that of a charged particle."

—*People*

"[Dr. Ruth's] manner is down-to-earth and reassuring . . . She tries to make people feel better, value themselves, and trust their instincts."

—*Ladies' Home Journal*

"Dr. Ruth writes the way she talks—enthusiastically, nonjudgmentally, and informatively."

—*Booklist*

"Her name and the distinctive thrill of her voice have become inextricably linked with the subject of sex."

—*New York Times*

Stay or Go

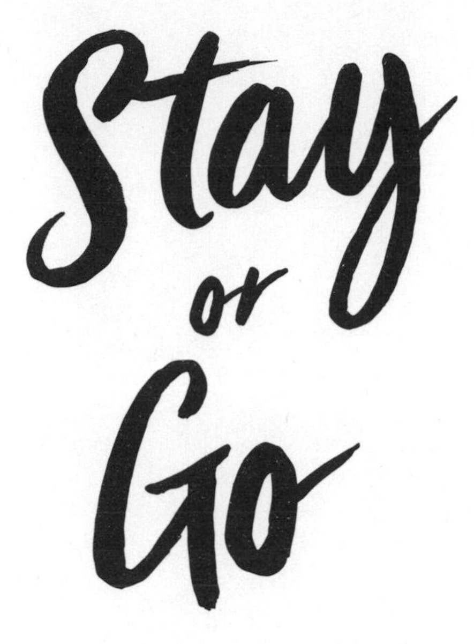

Dr. Ruth's Rules for Real Relationships

DR. RUTH K. WESTHEIMER

WITH PIERRE A. LEHU

amazon publishing

Published by Amazon Publishing, New York

www.apub.com

ISBN-13: 9781542046718
ISBN-10: 1542046718

Cover design by Faceout Studio

Printed in the United States of America

To all those who are sitting on a fence

"Go forward from here for your benefit and your good."

—Rashi on commentary in Genesis on God's command to Abraham

CONTENTS

INTRODUCTION

Although I'm best known as a sex therapist, I've done my share of marital and relationship therapy. What I find the most frustrating is when a couple comes to see me when it's already too late to fix the relationship. Therapists don't possess superpowers. Those of us with the proper training and experience can be helpful in repairing a damaged relationship, but if the people involved already have drifted too far apart, then we can't do anything.

Of course, some couples never should have gotten together in the first place, so trying to turn them into a loving couple would have been a waste of time from day one. Understanding what you're getting into is the subject for another book—which, by the way, I will be writing. In this book, I'm sticking to the subject of deciding whether your current relationship can be salvaged. Sometimes it can, and, sadly, sometimes it can't.

When I had my radio show and a caller recounted his or her tale of woe concerning a partner, if I determined the relationship was hopeless, I would point to my producer Susan Brown, who sat on the other side of the studio's glass. This was her cue her to play a snippet of the song "I'm Gonna Wash That Man Right Outa My Hair" from the Broadway show *South Pacific*.

As a therapist, I truly believe in putting time and effort into making a relationship work, not because I'm a hopeless romantic, but because

I've helped many couples salvage their relationships. I'm also a realist, so I know in certain situations the best decision you can make is to cut your losses.

This book is for you and not about me; however, I want to share an important part of my philosophy right up front. I've come close to losing my life a few times. First, I escaped the Holocaust by being sent to an orphanage in Switzerland. Then, as a messenger for the Israeli underground during the War of Independence, I was always at risk of being shot, and I was seriously wounded in a bomb blast in Jerusalem in which several people standing next to me were killed. My life experiences have taught me how precious life is, so I try not to waste any of mine.

Of course, you shouldn't need a near-death experience to appreciate how valuable every single minute is, though it helps. You've probably seen people stuck in a situation—a close romantic relationship, a friendship, a job, membership in an organization—in which it's clear they need to move on and yet they don't. The most common reaction of someone outside such a situation is to ask the person, "Why keep torturing yourself?" That's a good question, but I'd pose it from a different angle: "Why waste even one second of the next act of your life?" In other words, as soon as you realize that the situation is hopeless, move on and prepare yourself for whatever or whomever is coming next. If your next romance is going to be a bliss-filled one and your current one has you crying your eyes out all the time, then why delay in starting the process of finding that new mate?

As you know, being presented with a stark black-or-white situation is rare. You probably like some parts of the relationship and not others. Figuring out in which direction the scales are tipping is what I hope I can help you to figure out.

My final thought before getting to the heart of the book's material has to do with whom you should listen to, or, in other words, why you should listen to me. If you had a sharp pain in your abdomen, would you rush to see your next-door neighbor, your sister, or the woman who does your nails? Of course not; you'd go to your doctor. What does your doctor have to offer that these other folks don't? Years of training and experience. Although a relationship that blows up might not have the same deadly consequence as your appendix rupturing, the concept is the same. The advice provided by your friends and family is going to be based strictly on their life experiences. Some of that advice may be applicable, but much of it won't be. More than likely, they'll offer some common sense, which can be useful, but they'll also likely make some erroneous suggestions that could worsen the situation.

As a therapist, I've undergone years of training. And the advice I give has undergone thorough road testing. If a couple comes to me and I tell them to do X, Y, or Z, and they report back to me that it worked, then I am confident about giving that advice again. More importantly, those who come to me can also be confident in my advice because I've seen that it's effective.

You don't need to bottle your emotions and maintain a strict zone of silence around yourself. In fact, talking about your troubles can be very comforting. Having close buddies to whom you can pour out your heart is great; just don't listen to their advice without carefully analyzing the potential consequences. If, for example, you're thinking of leaving someone and all your friends say that doing so is the right move, then that probably will give you comfort in your decision. But if you're unsure of what to do, be careful about heeding the feedback you get, because it may be biased in a variety of ways that could lead you to make the wrong decision.

As you read this book, you're going to see questions that I've dubbed **"Stop and Consider."** When you encounter one of them, please stop reading and take some time to consider that question. The placement of these questions is important, because they directly relate to the current topic. The goal is to give you a knowledge base about your relationship.

Making some notes about your answers may be helpful. Not every question will apply to you, but thinking about each one may still be useful to your situation.

I'll address some of the material in these questions in the chapters at the end of the book, but I want to make sure that you use this valuable tool as you're reading.

1.

An Overview of Relationship Issues

You experience a sharp pain in your abdomen, see a doctor, and are told that it's appendicitis. Soon you're in a hospital bed, missing your appendix. And by missing, I mean physically missing because the doctor has surgically removed it. It's all pretty straightforward, assuming there aren't any complications.

Extracting yourself from a relationship isn't as easy. You have no emotional ties to your appendix, so after the pain of the surgery goes away, your brain doesn't keep sounding a red alert each time you pass that hospital. But when it comes to that bar where you first met a significant other—well, that's another story, isn't it?

If you think way back, about that little girl or boy on whom you had a crush in first grade, you still feel an emotional twinge of some sort. You might not care about anyone else in that class, but you wonder what this crush looks like now and whether he or she is single or married, fat or skinny, rich or poor. And that's true even if you never kissed. You can't simply erase the emotional ties you create when your heart is involved. They leave behind scars on your psyche that are always with you. You have to look in a mirror or at your body to see physical scars, but emotional scars can pop into your head at any time and over and over again. (Just think of how often people from your past pop into your dreams.) Regardless of whether you've ever experienced a bad breakup, you probably can appreciate how painful tearing yourself away from someone you once loved can be, which is why people instinctively hesitate before ending a relationship.

> **Dr. Ruth Westheimer**
> @AskDrRuth
>
> Breaking up is hard to do because severing all ties is impossible.

If the process of moving on is going to bring you a world of pain, why undergo it? Sadly, too many people decide the answer is "I won't." I say "sadly" because over time the cumulative pain of staying in a toxic relationship is likely to be worse than the awful feelings that come with a big breakup. Yet the path of least resistance beckons strongly.

Stop and Consider: Are you following the path of least resistance or doing what's right for you?

One reason for taking the path of least resistance is hope. If you're stuck in a relationship with someone who overall isn't right for you, there's a good chance that you saw his or her faults much earlier but hoped that you could build up the positive aspects and minimize the negative ones. Now, though, a lot of time has passed, and the changes you hoped for haven't happened. I'm not one to say that change is impossible. However, change isn't a likely occurrence if it's based only on hope. You might be able to induce change with a well-thought-out plan, but merely hoping for change isn't a well-thought-out plan.

> **Dr. Ruth Westheimer**
> @AskDrRuth
>
> Hoping for improvement isn't a plan.

When couples are in trouble, they usually come in three different flavors:

- Dark Toxic: They shouldn't stay together for one more second.
- Rocky Road: They've hit a rough patch and have arrived at an intersection. Whether they will find their way back to a wholesome relationship is unclear.
- Merely Troubled: Their love is still strong, but in today's world, where so many couples don't last, they're not sure how to proceed.

Stop and Consider: What type of relationship are you in?

Whatever situation a couple find themselves in, they need a plan. Relationship issues, if left to fester, will only get worse. I'll be offering advice on what your plan should include throughout the book. For now, my point is that chance alone isn't going to be your salvation. Yes, a few people do win the lottery, but the majority don't. You can't just sit and watch the minutes, hours, days, or years tick by. You have to set limits and make decisions about what you will do when you reach those limits.

> **Dr. Ruth Westheimer**
> @AskDrRuth
>
> Put an egg timer filled with sand on your desk to remind you not to let your relationship suck the life out of you one grain at a time.

Making plans to fix your relationship doesn't guarantee success. Your plans may be flawed, or the person sharing your life may be too stubborn, fragile, or damaged to work with those plans. Making and implementing plans also has a downside: it makes you vulnerable. Diving into the pool means it's sink or swim, which can be a lot scarier than standing by the edge. So what can you do to reduce the fear of failure?

Stop and Consider: Are you afraid of trying because you're afraid of failing?

The first thing to do is to take off your rose-colored glasses. In other words, take a closer look at your relationship. Are you really risking a lot by stirring the pot, or are you instead more afraid of appearing foolish or having to publicly admit you made a mistake? Some fears are worthy of the emotional stress they cause, while others aren't. Understanding exactly what's at risk might make the task easier. If, on examination, you conclude your relationship is of the Dark Toxic variety, then making plans to abandon ship won't be that hard to do.

How do you conduct this self-analysis? You need pencil and paper. If you do it in your head, you risk focusing on the same items on your list again and again. Yes, that fight you had last Tuesday was a bad one, but this assessment you're undertaking isn't about one battle but the entire war. If you make the list on your smartphone or computer, you risk your partner finding it, but make sure to put the handwritten list somewhere it won't be found accidentally. And making the list isn't something you can do in a few moments. Your brain needs time to digest these thoughts. Pace yourself. Take ten minutes here and fifteen minutes there and write down whatever comes to mind, including the good and the bad. After a few sessions, it's likely that patterns will appear, whether mostly positive or mostly negative. You're searching for patterns rather than specifics, because looking at patterns will lead you to the path you need to take.

Stop and Consider: What's the pattern of your relationship path?

Of course, putting your relationship under the microscope is scary by nature. Doing so may be the obvious move, but many people put it off. In fact, many couples won't go for any type of therapy, because they don't want to examine their relationships so closely. The very act of stepping into a therapist's office, or even calling to make an appointment, is a commitment to change. You're about to reveal the true nature of your feelings for your partner to a professional who has seen it all. You're going to get some feedback from someone who knows what he or she is talking about, and you might not like what you're going to hear. You're going to get pushed toward either improving the relationship or ending it, and maybe the seeming safety of standing still has you in its grips. A therapist doesn't have the ability to force you to take action, but after you've invested in therapy, talking yourself out of taking steps will be more difficult. As a result, some people choose the path of least resistance, which is to not step foot into that office in the first place.

One problem that therapists encounter is that their clients are prone to giving them only half of the facts. They may paint a rosy picture or else make their partner seem like a monster. A therapist can't give you useful advice if he or she is seeing a doctored image rather than the real picture. It's easier to lie to a therapist than to lie to yourself, but it's not impossible. If you're afraid of the truth, you can "forget" to share important moments, like the time he shoved you or when she embarrassed you in front of your family. In either case, whether talking to a therapist or yourself, be completely honest. The truth might hurt in the short run but not as much as it will to stay with someone you don't belong with in the long run.

Stop and Consider: Are you lying to yourself about your relationship?

People say there are no guarantees, but that's not entirely true. If you stay in a relationship that's making you miserable, you're guaranteed to be miserable. If you leave it, you're guaranteed to feel the pain that comes from snipping those ties that bind you to this other person. You aren't guaranteed that your efforts to make repairs to your relationship will improve it—at least not to the point where you want to remain in it.

> **Dr. Ruth Westheimer**
> @AskDrRuth
>
> Toasters come with guarantees; relationships don't.

Then there are the really sad cases, the ones in which a partner leaves only to return months, weeks, or even just days later. Being in a yo-yo relationship is the worst scenario of all, because you can never really enjoy the ups, knowing that the next down is right around the corner. If you recognize that is what's happening to you, then cut the string forever.

Stop and Consider: Are you in a yo-yo relationship?

Hard to shake loose from a longtime romantic relationship, you say? Here's a tip to make it a little easier to bear: try developing a crush on a celebrity. When your brain conjures up that partner you've just left or are about to leave, switch your thinking to some fantasy about this celebrity. You can even put up some pictures of this person around you. (You're a fan, so who's going to question this?) The point of this type of exercise is to train your brain not to keep your thoughts lingering on this toxic partner of yours. And choosing a celebrity as your fantasy lover is better than choosing someone who might be available, like a coworker or neighbor. Selecting someone close to you might make you feel guilty and confuse you when you're making this decision to leave. A celebrity who is unavailable won't include such hazards.

> **Dr. Ruth Westheimer**
> @AskDrRuth
>
> Fantasies can be useful tools to train your brain not to keep fixating on negative thoughts.

Intertwining your life with someone else means there is never going to be an easy way out. For instance, say that you're in a bad marriage and you both decide to go for therapy. After six months of your weekly sessions, you may have progressed into what can best be described as a tolerable marriage. Is "tolerable" good enough to stay together? What if instead you could be in a great marriage? Only you can answer those questions, and whether to stay in a so-so marriage can sometimes be the hardest decision to make. You've worked at the marriage and made improvements, and if you leave it, you'd not only have to justify this move to yourself and your partner, who put some effort into making repairs, but also to your friends and family.

This is one reason to keep private relationship matters private: you can make up your mind without an audience. If you confide your marital problems to friends and family, you'll have to deal with various types of peer pressure. Having to explain yourself to others can cause decision-making to be more difficult. If the tipping point of making this decision isn't obvious, peer pressure might force you into making the wrong choice. And because peer pressure works on your subconscious, you might not even realize the effect it had on *your* decision.

Stop and Consider: Is peer pressure influencing your decision-making?

I understand the need to talk to people you trust about your problems. But if you're going to open your heart, at least don't reveal every little detail. You may have this need for emotional release, but don't go overboard. Hold back information that people outside your relationship might not entirely understand. For example, say that he leaves his dirty laundry on the floor for you to pick up. You have a big fight about it. The next day you pour your heart out to your best friend, moaning about how much this bad habit annoys you. But then he takes you out for a romantic dinner, and you spend the commute to work the next morning dreamily thinking about how much you love him, so you decide that this one quirk isn't enough to cause a split. However, every time you see your friend, she asks you if he's still leaving his clothes around. You've decided to live with it, but she makes you feel guilty, driving a wedge between you and him. Now because I believe in white lies, in that situation my advice would be to tell your friend that he's magically been transformed into a neatnik. My point is to be extremely careful what you say to friends and family so that you don't find yourself painted into a corner.

Stop and Consider: Do you tell every little detail about your relationship to one or more friends? If so, what impact might that have on your decision-making?

Spreading bad news about your partner can have ramifications. If your partner is certain that you told your best friend about this fight, he will figure that if he starts picking up his clothes, she's going to know about that, too. He may feel that his masculinity is threatened by *her* reaction. Although he might be talked into changing this habit because he loves you and understands how unfair it is, backing down from your entire circle of friends could be more than his ego can handle.

Of course, this situation could escalate. Now instead of just fighting about his dirty socks, you're fighting about your friends. Perhaps when he finds out that you've aired your relationship dirty laundry in front of them, he no longer wants to have anything to do with them. But they're an important part of your social life, so now there's a whole new layer of issues to settle between the two of you.

Dr. Ruth Westheimer
@AskDrRuth

You might trigger hidden agendas by making your private life public.

The reason there are no guarantees when it comes to fixing relationships is that they're so complicated. More complicated than you might even realize. Unless you've undergone years of psychotherapy, you're likely unaware of what aspects of your past affect how you react to various psychological stimuli today. For instance, maybe your father left his underwear on the floor for your mom to pick up, and he also caused the bruises you would see on her arms. In that case, your current partner's annoying habit of leaving his laundry on the floor could have a much more serious effect on you than either of you could imagine. While you might be unaware of some of your own emotional triggers, knowing all your partner's emotional triggers is impossible. After all, you've spent only a relatively short time with this person. You have a partial picture of your partner's psychological makeup. You know some of the buttons but not all of them. You can't fully understand your own motivations, let alone those of your partner, and this means you can navigate a relationship only in broad strokes, dealing with major issues while allowing minor ones to go unaddressed. Fine-tuning is more likely to fail, because there are obstacles out there that you can't see but that still have an impact on your relationship.

Stop and Consider: What in your past might be affecting how you react to your partner?

Emotions are bound to play a strong role in a romantic relationship. However, you have to rationally decide whether to stay or go; otherwise, you might pack your bags at the end of the next argument you have. Whatever you do, don't make decisions when emotions are high;

doing so will increase the odds of making a rash decision that you will regret later.

> **Dr. Ruth Westheimer**
> @AskDrRuth
>
> Don't make decisions when you're in a highly emotional state.

Another mistake you might make is to fall for the concept of soul mates, two people who are perfectly matched. This idea can be dangerous because it puts impossible pressure on the couple: every relationship is flawed in some way or another. No one is perfect, and two people sharing their lives can multiply imperfections. When you have two people making decisions, then even simple choices, in which neither partner is right or wrong, can cause conflict. There are always going to be those he-likes-the-bedroom-window-open, she-likes-it-closed moments. They're unavoidable, and they spoil the ideal of perfection. Rather than thinking, *He can't really be my soul mate if he insists on leaving the window open all night when he knows I like it closed,* it's better to accept that your relationship isn't going to be perfect and learn the art of compromise. (When it comes to snoring, which is a common bedroom issue, I'm a big believer in the compromise of having separate bedrooms!)

> **Dr. Ruth Westheimer**
> @AskDrRuth
>
> The concept of having a soul mate leads only to disappointment.

The other problem with expecting perfection is that it doesn't allow for change. Say that several of your friends split with their partners, and they all agreed that one of the major problems they had was that they couldn't find enough time to connect. They were so busy that sometimes it was days or even weeks between the times they really sat down and talked. This lack of communication made their relationship weaker and weaker. Hearing these tales makes you so thankful that this can't happen to you, because you and your partner work near to one another and get to talk during your morning commute. And then a headhunter calls with a job that will double your salary but is on the opposite side of town.

You have a keen appreciation for the need for regular communication, because what happened to your friends is an important lesson. But taking this new job doesn't have to be the end of good communication or put your relationship at risk. You and your partner just have to find new opportunities to talk. If you think about it, much of what you talked about during your commute was probably fluff, so you don't necessarily have to create an hour a day out of thin air. It's also true that most serious conversations do take some time to develop, so you can't expect to squeeze the same level of communication into five minutes. You'll have to compromise and find some time during the week to keep essential communication going.

> **Dr. Ruth Westheimer**
> @AskDrRuth
>
> Write down thoughts you want to pass on to your partner. Then when you do find a moment to talk, you won't forget what you wanted to say.

Of course, it's easier for me to say that you must find the time to communicate than for you to find that time. I suggest that in discussing whether to take this job with your partner, you immediately try to figure out when you will communicate going forward. Let your partner know how important this job is to you and that you'll make a priority of staying in touch. Couples are going to have to find their own solutions, but if they're serious, then doing so won't be that hard (though it might mean a little less sleep!). And you can't rule out the possibility that this new job will come not only with a higher pay but also with a higher level of responsibility that in turn might add other stresses to your relationship. But if you assume the worst, if you say to yourself, *We're never going to survive this*, then you won't. Life is going to throw you a wide assortment of challenges, especially if you ever have children. If you go around enamored of your perfect little world, thinking it provides a safety net, then you'd better disavow yourself of that notion and learn how to build a relationship that can withstand imperfections and difficulties. Prepare to be flexible, resilient, and willing to compromise. Be ready to fight for your loving relationship.

At the opposite end of the spectrum of soul mates are the Romeos and Juliets, the star-crossed lovers who the fates dictated couldn't last as a couple. All couples have good days and bad days, but if the two of you always seem to have a dark cloud over your head, don't blame the fates. Maybe you're not suited to each other. Perhaps you're not trying hard enough or working on the relationship, and instead you're allowing your relationship to drift onto the rocks. You might not be able to fully control your life, but don't negate the control that is available. You're neither soul mates nor star-crossed lovers, which is why the decision of whether to stay together or not is in your hands.

This advice applies to couples in a committed relationship, and if you're married, don't forget the standard marriage vows, when you promise you're going to stick together for better or worse, richer or poorer, in sickness and in health. How important are those vows (or simply the commitment to be a monogamous couple) to you? With something like 50 percent of all marriages ending in divorce, saying vows in front of friends and family obviously isn't a guarantee that you will stay married forever. To me, however, the most important aspect of these vows is the commitment to put in your best effort to work out whatever problems might arise. Admittedly those problems might be so serious that they overwhelm your commitment. But if you don't make that commitment in the first place, then it won't take much of a headwind to split you apart.

Stop and Consider: How important to you is the commitment you made to your partner?

So far in this book, I haven't written much about love. Of course, love is important, but in arranged marriages, which have been widespread throughout history and continue in many cultures today, love has nothing to do with marriage. Many of these arranged marriages thrive. Is it something about these other cultures, or is love not as important as we in our society make it seem?

Love is a key ingredient. In an emotional vacuum with no love, the odds increase that somewhere along the way one or both partners in a loveless marriage may end up falling in love with someone else to fill that void, which isn't going to make for a happy marriage. Hence, love needs to be integrated into the committed relationship for it to be strong and lasting. But love also complicates matters because of some of its attributes. Love can make you blind. You can fall in love with someone who is mean, nasty, overbearing, and worse. Knowing that love isn't enough is important. You also need to be clearheaded when making a commitment, and love sometimes surrounds its victims in a dense fog.

Stop and Consider: Could you be blinded by love?

Even though there's a certain kind of love that the French call *le coup de foudre*, which translates literally as "the bolt of lightning" and describes love at first sight, love also can grow slowly and steadily. Certainly, couples who are in an arranged marriage come to love each other very deeply.

This term, "love," has many different meanings to different people. Love is an emotion that evolves over time, and sometimes from day to day. The Beatles once sang the lyrics, "Love has a nasty habit of disappearing overnight," and that situation can be as true as love that lasts forever. Although love is certainly a strong attractant, it's not necessarily a clear indication of whether two people belong together or whether they will live happily ever after. You can be blinded by love and believe strongly that the person you're with is perfect, but something can pop that bubble of love, and then you will discover that he or she is the last person with whom you'd want to spend the rest of your life.

We've reached the crux of the problem: How do you make sure that the person you love is Mr. or Ms. Right for you?

Obviously, you can never be 100 percent sure, because change is an integral part of life. To cite a common example, two people are in a seemingly happy relationship, then the main wage earner loses his or her job, and the ensuing financial difficulties drive an enormous wedge between the two. That's just one of dozens of complications that can doom a relationship. So let's put that goal of 100 percent certitude to the side.

For many people, doing just that is an important first step. Some people worry so much about the distant future that they become paralyzed by all the potential what-ifs. For example, you know your partner had an uncle who was an alcoholic, so you worry, *What if he turns into one?* If he doesn't seem to overindulge now, worrying he might become an alcoholic in the future, when that might never happen, is foolish, and it might prevent you from committing.

If he has alcoholism in his family and he does tend to drink a lot, then that's another story. Don't ignore actual risks. Just ignore those that have such a low potential of happening that they are only distracting you from making the best choice.

<u>Stop and Consider:</u> What assumptions do you have about your partner that might not be true?

Let me say something about emotional reactions at this point. You can't prevent emotional reactions. For example, say that your partner hires a new associate who used to be a male model, and you've never been confident about your looks. You drop into the office and meet him and feel jealous, even though as far as you know, there's no reason to be jealous. Can you prevent yourself from experiencing the emotion of jealousy in the moment? No, you can't. But what happens next is crucial to your relationship.

If you allow a negative emotion like jealousy to fester, it's going to harm your relationship. Because you can't stop such emotions from making cameo appearances, you have to develop the skills to deflect them so that they become harmless. When you feel jealous, think back on a favorite moment you spent with your partner, maybe your honeymoon. Force those feelings of jealousy out of your mind by replacing them with sweet memories of good times. Doing so will diminish the ability of negative emotions to cause damage. If you successfully push these thoughts aside when you begin to sense them, after a while, your brain will stop sending messages of jealousy.

> **Dr. Ruth Westheimer**
> @AskDrRuth
>
> You can't control emotions, but you can control how strong an effect they have on you.

I keep a drawer full of letters that made me happy when I first read them. If I feel sad, I reach into that drawer and read a couple of the letters, and they lift my spirits. Here's another time to reflect on some of your favorite moments with your partner. Consider keeping a notebook in which you record some of the good times the two of you have shared. Then if you need something to cheer you or distract you from negative thoughts, you can reach for your "rainy day" notebook.

However, some emotional reactions are essential. For example, if someone you care about deeply passes away, you need to mourn. You have to allow yourself to feel those sad emotions. There's no set time period—whatever is right for you varies depending on the circumstances. Any attempts to be selective when stopping emotions can be quite damaging. In order to successfully stuff one emotion in a corner of your brain, you have no choice but to close off your brain to all emotions. By not allowing yourself to feel sad at the death of a loved one, you'll end up not allowing yourself to feel love either. To reiterate, you have to deflect any emotions that are clearly negative, like unwarranted jealousy, so that they don't cause any damage. The trick is to deflect these negative emotions rather than shut down all your emotions.

Stop and Consider: Are you blocking all your emotions because you're trying to protect yourself from one of them?

A culling process needs to take place to be able to know which worries are worthy of attention and which ones aren't. To return to my earlier example, if you're worried about alcoholism, then you shouldn't merely push it aside. First, you have to rationally look at this risk and come to some conclusion. Is it a real danger or not? If you decide it's not a danger, then every time you start to worry about it, force yourself to think of something else. Don't try to stop these worries from cropping up, because you can't. The more you try, the more such thoughts are likely to pop up. Instead, when such a worry arises, tell yourself it's nonsense because you've never seen him drunk. After a while, that particular worry will stop causing you a problem.

> **Dr. Ruth Westheimer**
> @AskDrRuth
>
> You can train your brain to parry negative thinking, but it won't happen unless you make a conscious effort.

If he does get drunk every now and then, the decision of whether this potential problem is worth breaking up over becomes more complicated. But if such decisions weren't at times complicated, you wouldn't be reading this book.

I must admit that I'm somebody who believes in gut reactions. Your "gut" may signal you far ahead of your brain. You may feel jealous for good reasons, even if they aren't all that clear in the moment. Several pieces of a puzzle that your conscious mind can't piece together may be rattling around inside your head, even though your subconscious mind has already solved the puzzle. Add together some flirtatious behavior with some late nights that didn't have a good explanation with a lie or two, and this combination may indicate that you really do have a reason to be jealous. You need to trust your gut, but you shouldn't trust it so much that you make a too-hasty decision. Use those gut instincts to become more aware, and then at some point initiate a discussion or, better yet, a series of discussions.

Earlier in this chapter I mentioned fear of failure. I've just covered some issues that could lead you to make a split. You still may be hesitating, because this common fear—that of failure—is tied up in your ego and sense of self-worth. I suggest you hold on to the thought that a relationship requires two people. A failed relationship doesn't mean that you've failed, even if you're partly to blame. The two of you may not be right for each other. In the end, holding on to a bad relationship can be a much bigger failure than letting it go.

Allow me to say something now that I'll say again and again: if you're not ready to give up on a relationship and feel you can't salvage it by yourself, get professional help.

2.

A Lesson in Compatibility

You know those compatibility tests you regularly see in magazines? I've got nothing against reading them or even taking them. Where I draw the line is in believing the results and the analysis. Consider what I'm saying: I've had couples come to see me in my office, and I knew the situation was hopeless before either one had opened their mouth. Their body language told the entire story. A magazine test doesn't account for body language or dozens of other factors.

So why aren't I telling you to avoid the compatibility tests like the plague? It's simple. They can provide you with an awareness that you need to change direction. I'm not saying you need to head for the exit door; just look up and see in which direction your ship is heading.

> **Dr. Ruth Westheimer**
> @AskDrRuth
>
> Taking a relationship test may not be proof of anything, but it can set you on the road to getting at the truth.

Going to see a marriage counselor or participating in couples therapy can be crucial for saving a relationship, which is why I continuously congratulate people for taking steps in that direction. Selecting the therapist, making the appointment, and walking through the door of the therapist's office aren't always easy tasks. But none of those actions can happen until you recognize that the problem you have is worthy of a therapist's help. Maybe taking that magazine quiz will start a chain reaction that will either save or end your relationship. Just be aware that it's only one baby step.

Stop and Consider: Might couples therapy help your relationship?

No relationship is perfect. Disagreements are going to arise. The question is whether these disagreements will become a problem. And if they do, does that problem pose a sufficiently serious danger to your relationship that you need to take action? The only way you're going to discover the answer is if you analyze your situation.

Being compatible doesn't mean that you match in every way. That's just not possible. Each of you has so many aspects to your personality that for each of them to dovetail perfectly is incredibly unlikely. Some personality traits carry so much weight that a relationship probably won't stand up to the test of time. Yes, some night owls marry early birds and still find time to meet, and May-December marriages can be quite successful, but too much difference might make every day an uphill battle. If the road you two travel together has occasional rough patches, that's fine, but if it's always like driving a horse and carriage down a cobblestone street, then the likelihood of a wheel falling off is pretty high.

To assess whether you two are compatible, you'll want to aim for a passing grade rather than an A+. This grade isn't based on a scientific study but on your personal feelings and your willingness to compromise.

To some degree every relationship is like a pearl. An oyster can't make a pearl without a grain of sand getting inside its shell and causing irritation. If you have a partner who is so blah that he or she doesn't cause any of your emotions to flare up even a little, then what might seem like a perfect relationship from the outside could be so boring that it drives you crazy. Just because you don't fight or bicker doesn't mean that your relationship is healthy. I'm not advocating fighting, mind you, but I give my sternest warnings regarding boredom, and not just in the bedroom. From my perspective, compatibility isn't a matter of your relationship being free from conflict; rather, it's that your relationship is full of life, which may or may not include some occasional conflict.

Stop and Consider: Are you bored with your relationship?

One way of answering this question is by looking at your desire to be with your partner. If you find yourself going out of your way to be anywhere other than together, then clearly you have a serious problem. You might have a boring partner or it might be something else altogether, but if you have little desire to spend time with your partner, then you have to take a serious look at your situation.

Stop and Consider: What is more desirable? Being with your partner or being wherever your partner isn't?

When assessing blahness, you also have to examine yourself. If you work and commute ten hours a day, more than likely you don't arrive home ready to go out salsa dancing. But if your favorite activity is to veg out in front of the TV, then ask yourself why your partner might want to share an evening with you. Vegging out occasionally to recharge your batteries is OK, but if every moment of your free time is spent on mindless activity, then don't be surprised if your partner changes his or her mind about your relationship.

> **Dr. Ruth Westheimer**
> @AskDrRuth
>
> Vegging out weakens relationships.

Here's the most important part about compatibility: it's adaptable, and by both parties. But only if you let each other know your desires. I always say that a man can't guess what a woman needs to have an orgasm. He could try a variety of ways of stimulating her, but he still might get it wrong, which wouldn't be his fault, because she may need a specific manner of being stimulated. She has to communicate what she needs to cause the orgasmic response. (And although I'm not against occasional faking, if a woman fakes it all the time, then she deserves the lack of sexual satisfaction.) But you respond to your partner in many more ways than just sexually. And what's true about sex is also true for the rest of what you do together. If you're unhappy about how the two of you spend your leisure hours, speak up! If your partner is unwilling to compromise, then maybe you're not compatible. If you keep silent, then your partner is going to assume that everything is fine. So judging compatibility requires responsibility on your part.

Stop and Consider: Do you speak up and tell your partner what your likes and dislikes are?

Returning to the soul mate obstacle, some people are under the impression that if their partner really loves them, he or she will instinctively know how to please them in every way. For example, you wanted to go to that romantic Italian restaurant Friday night, so he should be able to read your desire over the airwaves. Granted, some people are extremely good at reading others, but just as many are clueless. Not being able to read your mind doesn't make your partner a terrible person or even a bad match. Deciding that your partner is intentionally ignoring your desires because he or she should just "know" how you feel by virtue of being your soul mate is nonsense. You have to proactively communicate your desires. Sometimes a hint is enough, and sometimes you need to hit your partner over the head with your request. Until you speak your mind and your partner actually turns you down, don't ever assume that your desires aren't being met.

Another specific area where it happens a lot is with presents. If you want a specific present for your birthday and you don't tell your partner, how can you possibly be disappointed if you're given something else? If you expect both a surprise and a specific present, you're setting up your partner for failure and yourself for disappointment. When deciding whether to stay in a relationship, it's unfair to measure your partner against unattainable goals.

Stop and Consider: Do you ever set yourself up for failure?

The next important point is that you have to know what you want. For instance, if you feel that your work life is stifling your creative juices and you need to devote some hours to painting, then figure out how to fit that in. Unless your partner poses for you, painting is a solitary activity, so you'd want to schedule this personal time and be sure to make time to do something else with your partner. Visiting museums and art galleries could be something you could do together and which would relate to your passion for painting.

That's where compatibility comes in. If you want to go to a museum and your partner absolutely refuses, even though he knows how much art means to you, then maybe you have an issue. One would think that there would be room for compromise: museum one day, jazz club (or whatever is important to your partner) another day. If your partner refuses to compromise in a situation like this, and this adds to a long list of other examples, then the two of you need to reexamine your relationship.

Stop and Consider: **Do you both compromise, or are you the only one who compromises?**

Right now, you might be wondering how you can determine if you're just being stubborn and making unreasonable demands. Looking inward and being objective can be difficult. I've heard top models say that they look at themselves in the mirror and think, *Yuck*. You need to examine your thoughts and actions in addition to those of your partner. In fact, if a breakup is on the horizon, make sure that you know how much you contributed to the breakup so that your next relationship will be based on more solid ground. It's rare that a relationship goes sour based on the actions of one half of the couple. Yes, one person may share more of the blame, but there's usually enough blame to go around.

If your partner is an alcoholic or an addict, is prone to violence, or is psychotic in some way, the previous sentence may not hold. You might have been bending over backward for years, but the outcome was never going to change, because your partner didn't have the self-control to make any improvements. And in such relationships, compatibility is hard to find, though something drew you together in the first place.

And don't stay in a relationship out of pity. Discovering your partner is an alcoholic is sad, but that discovery doesn't mean you need to remain a couple. You could suggest treatment, but if your partner refuses, then that's a "Get Out of Jail Free" card as far as I'm concerned.

Stop and Consider: **Are you remaining in the relationship out of pity for your partner?**

There is also the concept of mercy. You discover, whether before or after you've formed a twosome, that this person has a serious fault or two. Some people will run away at the first sign of a problem. They refuse to look beyond this problem to see if there are qualities that make such a relationship worth having regardless. Sometimes showing compassion can be rewarding. Some relationships require more effort. By seeking the deeper aspects of this seemingly flawed person, you might benefit greatly.

Let me tell you a quick story. I was teaching human sexuality at Brooklyn College, and one of my classes was specifically geared to people with disabilities. I said I would never do that again. Why? I gained so much from that class that I wanted to share what I had learned with all students, mixing people with disabilities and without in one course.

Stop and Consider: Have you examined your relationship below the surface carefully enough?

If you happen to form a relationship with someone who has an imperfection or two, look beneath the surface before you head for the hills. You might find the makings of a relationship that would be well worth holding on to.

Some people confuse compatibility with love or lust. You can be madly in love with the wrong person, and you can be extremely turned on by someone who should never be your partner. So how do you determine what's going on? You can't always notice in the early stages of a relationship, but as the relationship develops, it's usually less and less difficult. Love and lust tend to lose some of their shininess after a while. These emotions don't necessarily weaken; they just become less blinding. And if the two of you have any compatibility issues, then after you've been together a bit longer, those issues start to become more apparent, and you have to pay more attention to them.

> **Dr. Ruth Westheimer**
> @AskDrRuth
>
> When love and lust start to wane a bit, take that as a reminder to reexamine your relationship.

I don't want to turn you into a robot that doesn't have any emotions and makes decisions by facts alone. Quite the contrary, love and lust should play an important role in how you choose a partner. But these emotions can blur the lines when it comes to discerning compatibility. How could you be incompatible with someone you love? Doesn't make sense, does it? Until you look more closely, that is.

Here's an example of why I say love alone doesn't prove compatibility. You can be in love with someone who doesn't love you back. Clearly the two of you are incompatible in that situation. In fact, you're not even a couple; you're driving the wrong way down a one-way street, which can lead only to a crash. That example is extreme, but if you've never had that happen to you, you most certainly know other people who've been in such situations—madly in love with someone who won't give them the time of day. The situation is pitiful, but you can't blame the person who's the target of these affections. He or she just doesn't have any of those feelings to return, and that's perfectly fine.

Today people have sex with friends—friends with benefits—so there's lust, at least enough for both parties to enjoy the sex, but they're not compatible enough to be in a relationship either, or else they'd become a couple.

Another common situation is when two people are very good friends, but they don't have any chemistry, so friends they remain, never becoming a couple. In this situation and the friends-with-benefits situation, too, sometimes one person is in love with the other, but the love is unrequited, a one-way-street love. To me it's very sad when that happens. Why? Because the person who is in love will waste a lot of time, maybe even years, hoping that the object of his or her affection might someday feel differently. Instead of being available to a real partner, the person stays glued to their "friend."

Dr. Ruth Westheimer
@AskDrRuth

Love and lust aren't enough to make you compatible.

This type of relationship in which two people spend lots of time together but never fall in love points out a dichotomy. Here you have two people, two friends, who, by definition, are compatible. If neither has a significant other, they may spend hours and hours sharing activities that bring them a lot of pleasure and enjoying themselves as much as a romantically linked couple. But because at least one of them doesn't have that emotional attachment, because there's no spark, the relationship isn't going to become romantic.

If you're a part of such a non-couple, you need to give serious consideration to "breaking up" or at least taking a breather. As long as you're leaning on this friend, you'll never find a real lover, especially if you have a strong emotional attachment to this person. I'm not saying that you can't remain friends and see each other occasionally, but if you're not readily available because you're seeing your friend, then finding a lover is just not going to be possible.

The recipe for a good relationship is like a casserole. You need different ingredients—love, lust, and compatibility—mixed together and cooked at the right temperature. Two people who might be incompatible, at least on some levels, still might be able to form a long-lasting and strong relationship if they have enough love and lust to hold them together.

What if the lust has disappeared entirely, and you don't want to have sex with your partner anymore? This can be an indication of a serious relationship problem, or it can be a false alarm. Women need a certain amount of time to become aroused. A man can have an erection in seconds, but that type of instant arousal rarely happens in women. If a woman has had a hard day at the office without even a second to think romantically about her partner, then they have a hurried dinner, then she needs to send ten e-mails for work before they go to bed, at which point he makes a sexual advance, she's almost definitely not going to be interested. She just hasn't had enough time to become aroused. So how do you distinguish between a lack of desire that is circumstantial and one that is specific to your partner?

The first thing I tell a woman in this situation is that, once in a while, it's good to go ahead and have sex even if you don't feel like it. The French have a saying that applies to food: *l'appétit vient en mangeant*, which roughly translates as "your appetite will come when eating." The same thing can apply to having sex. Maybe you didn't want to have sex, but after a certain amount of foreplay you become aroused and then end up having a fabulous orgasm. If that happens, your initial lack of appetite probably was circumstantial. But if you never want to have sex, even on a quiet weekend evening, and the thought of sex with your partner isn't attractive or is maybe even revolting, then you have a serious problem.

Stop and Consider: If your sex life has petered out, is it circumstantial or personal?

Another component that's important is trust. In most relationships, trust isn't an issue—well, that is, until it is an issue. Certainly, in the beginning of a relationship, when things are hot and heavy, the assumption is that if you're both always together, then cheating can't take place. But after a while, the other partner is going to notice any evidence of possible cheating. And if trust evaporates, that probably will spell the end of the relationship.

Sometimes the issue of trust crops up without any negative evidence. If several of your closest friends have ended a relationship because their partner cheated, you might be hyperaware of evidence of cheating, so that you become overly suspicious of your partner. A few late nights working, that before you would have ignored, might now seem suspect.

As I stated earlier, listening to your gut instinct is important. If you think your partner is cheating, then take some action. At the very least raise the issue in a serious conversation. Just remember that your brain is sensitive to outside influences. For example, you might not be afraid to fly, but if there's a major airplane crash on the day before you're due to fly, it's likely you're going to be more nervous than you would be ordinarily. What happened to those friends of yours with the cheating partners will affect you, so be aware of it. If you start acting needlessly jealous, you could cause a rift that wasn't there to begin with. Hence, trust is a key element in any relationship, but ideally one that you each can lock away somewhere deep in your psyche.

Stop and Consider: Do you fully trust your partner, and if not, why not?

Relationships aren't fixed. Two people may be perfectly matched at a particular time in their lives and then later end up not as well matched. And those major factors in a relationship—love, lust, trust, and compatibility—can also increase or decrease. What you considered a loveable quirk in a partner when your love was overpowering may become a major source of annoyance if your love has weakened, even if only a bit. Then, each time your partner exhibits that quirk, it may weaken your love even more.

All relationships change. As you grow older and more mature, your relationship has to keep up. Just look at your taste in music. At one time, certain tunes made your ears perk up when they came on the radio. If those same tunes ended up on your playlist today, you'd quickly press the "Skip" button. And if you and your partner have been together for ten years and you had a *Twilight Zone* experience in which you walked into a bar and met your partner when he or she was ten years younger, do you think your heart would still skip a beat, or would you take a pass? For argument's sake, say that you wouldn't want to date that younger version of your partner, and the reason is that you've changed over that ten-year span. Returning to real life, you've changed but your partner hasn't changed, or he or she has changed in a different direction. You can start to see why your relationship might not be one you want to stay in.

Stop and Consider: Have you and your partner changed in ways that make you less compatible?

Sometimes there's no observable change on the outside, but the inside is another story. Objectively the relationship seems in good shape, but you're not really into it anymore. You long for the excitement that your partner used to provide, and you don't understand why it's gone.

It may not be gone. Maybe your busy life has masked it, which certainly is a possibility, so dig a little deeper into how you feel. Are you even allowing yourself to feel, or is the rush of your life forcing you to constantly hold your breath?

The reality may be that as the song goes, "the thrill is gone." So the next question is, can the thrill be brought back? If, after really trying, you just can't get that old mojo back, then maybe the day's arrived to end the relationship.

Are you at the point of making the decision to leave or stay? You're in a relationship that has some of the right ingredients; it has some love, some lust, and some compatibility, and yet you're not sure. Should any amount of doubt be sufficient reason to move on? And if there is a threshold, what the heck is it?

One way of deciding is to understand how much of a negative effect your relationship is having on the rest of your life. When you're at work, do you lose concentration because the state of your relationship keeps intruding? Are you losing sleep worrying about your relationship? If you're reading a book, do you have to stop every few paragraphs because thoughts about your relationship interrupt you? Has your appetite been affected? Have your favorite foods lost their appeal? Do you ever find yourself having difficulties breathing because of these worries? Have you been drinking more alcohol or taking any drugs to help you to calm down? If these symptoms or similar ones are affecting you, then you need to address the problem. It doesn't mean that you have to part ways with your partner, but it does mean that you have to act.

<u>Stop and Consider:</u> Is your relationship having a negative effect on the rest of your life?

There are many reasons why people in an anxiety-causing situation sit on their hands instead of taking action, whether for a short time, a long time, or even forever. Some prefer to be in a bad relationship rather than to be single. Perhaps they haven't had that many relationships in their life and decide that a bad relationship is better than no relationship.

<u>Stop and Consider:</u> Are you staying in a relationship in order not to be single?

Some individuals who decide to stay in a relationship are forced into it. I get letters from women saying that they want out of their relationship but leaving their partner is impossible for financial reasons. A woman who has always been a housewife may not have the skills to get a job that will pay enough for her to support herself. And having children will complicate her financial situation.

Then there are people who hang on to a relationship out of a fear of embarrassment, especially if they recently had a big, fancy, and costly wedding. They feel guilty if their parents put up the money and possibly ashamed with regard to anyone who gave them a gift. Unless a partner is caught cheating, the other person in the couple will know that everyone will question the sudden change of heart, because that's what he or she would do in similar circumstances.

Many people aren't psychologically prepared to make any major decisions, preferring to just put them off. And divorce has been shown in various studies to be the second-most mentally traumatic event after the death of a loved one. (The same would apply, it seems to me, to a long-term relationship that breaks apart.) Even someone with a great psychological makeup is going to shy away from such suffering.

However, if you're already on shaky ground, you can easily become afraid of falling apart completely because of a bad breakup.

Stop and Consider: Are you emotionally strong enough to go through a breakup?

If your relationship is rocky, then I suggest that you go to couples therapy. If your own mental state is unsteady, you could go to individual therapy. You might still need couples therapy, but it will be more productive if you're in a better place individually.

Family pressure is another factor holding many people back. Even though divorce is fairly common these days, it's still an admission of failure. And even if you're confident that divorce is the right decision, your family members might not agree, and their reaction could add to your misery. If you're having trouble deciding what to do, believing that your family won't support a split could make you stay with your partner.

Stop and Consider: How much is the potential reaction of your family keeping you from deciding to leave?

Just because divorce is common doesn't mean that someone who is divorced is looked at the same as someone who isn't. Even though the divorce might not primarily have been your fault, some individuals might see you as damaged goods. I'm not saying that you are, but you can't ignore the fact that this status will make future partners look you over more carefully. (Wouldn't you be more cautious about forming a relationship with a new partner who was divorced?)

Some of you stay in a relationship out of pity, because you know that a breakup would devastate your partner. This situation is more likely when your partner isn't eliciting the chemical reaction that he or she once did than when the relationship has more serious problems.

However, anyone contemplating a split would have to weigh in the partner's reaction. After all, you did love each other in the past, and you probably still care about your partner. If your partner is in any way psychologically unstable, his or her potential reaction to a breakup might become a factor in keeping you together.

I could give more examples, but my point is that separating isn't easy. Whatever the forces are that are pulling you apart, there are also forces keeping you together. Saying goodbye takes some effort, and some pain is going to be involved, probably a lot of pain, so you need to have a good case for going your separate ways. That's why trying to make repairs is so important. Repairing a relationship isn't always possible, but if it is, you and your partner can save yourselves a lot of pain and grief and a whole raft of other negative emotions.

> **Dr. Ruth Westheimer**
> @AskDrRuth
>
> Don't make the decision to leave without making every effort to stay together.

If you look at the two of you as you are now and can easily see that you're not compatible, is there any reason to attempt repairs? There could be several. You are never going to completely cut every single tie with this person. Even if he moves ten thousand miles away and you never ever communicate again, there will likely be moments when you're going to look him up on Facebook or LinkedIn. If you leave without making some effort to keep the two of you together, you're always going to wonder if you did the right thing. You're going to suffer from some guilt. But if you try to make it work and it doesn't (even when your efforts were doomed from the start and you absolutely knew it), there will be less guilt, and whatever feelings you have when someone who looks like him walks in front of you won't be quite as bad.

So even if you absolutely know it's not going to work out, you need to make the effort for your own peace of mind. I would say the less likely the chances of the relationship working, the less you need to do, but you need to take some action.

If you're looking for a written test from me that is going to determine your compatibility with your partner, you're not going to find it, because I don't believe it could ever be accurate. My reason is simple: compatibility is a judgment call. One woman might find it very important that her man be taller than she, while another couldn't care less. One man might need to find a partner who laughs at his jokes, while another might not. My husband was always telling jokes that went right over my head, and we were married for thirty-five years before he suddenly passed away. The "Stop and Consider" questions are for guidance, not to offer a final answer as to whether you should stay or go.

You're not going to find someone who is the perfect fit. You can't design your ideal partner and find him or her on Amazon. So you must weigh dozens of factors. I think what is important in judging compatibility is that some factors can be altered and some can't. A woman who decides she can't be with a man who is shorter than she should leave that shorter man. He's never going to grow. She might have thought she could overlook this physical characteristic of his, but if she can't, then that's that. Of course, people can improve themselves mentally. Let's say you marry someone who didn't go to college, and you find that when you're with your friends, all of whom are college graduates, you're ashamed of your spouse's remarks because he or she is undereducated. That's a fixable situation. Even without going to college, by reading a lot, anyone can improve their level of conversation. If your partner is willing to make that effort, then you might have found a real gem. Starting the discussion is not going to be easy, but it's better to talk about your concern than let it fester to the point of causing a breakup.

> **Dr. Ruth Westheimer**
> @AskDrRuth
>
> Difficult conversations to have are often the most important ones.

Compatibility really begins with you, not your partner. How picky are you? Everyone has faults, but if you're the type of person who can't overlook imperfections, then you might have to break up with a partner who continuously pushes one of your buttons. Of course, if you're too picky, you might never be able to find a partner, so that might be something you need to work on before you start looking again.

Stop and Consider: How picky are you? How much of a perfectionist are you?

To some degree, you can judge compatibility before you start dating a person, especially if you've already made a list of what is important to you. If you've been burned a few times, some items will jump to the top, like too much drinking or bigoted parents. Such a list helps create a sorting process that will save you time and possibly heartache. For example, if you absolutely won't marry someone of another religion, why even begin a relationship with someone who doesn't share your religion? Why set yourself up for a painful breakup? Because soul mates don't exist, I'm certain that you could meet someone just as compatible who also shares your religious beliefs, so narrow your search pool right away. If your list of absolute musts is too long, you might live a lonely life. As you make the list, see if you can make some compromises. Maybe he doesn't have to be taller than you if at least he's not shorter. Maybe she can have small breasts if she likes your favorite sports team. Be aware that when you start combining these nonnegotiables, you approach the level of impossibility already set by the soul-mate standard. My advice: for each characteristic you must have (say, religion), subtract another (say, height). That way your chances of meeting with success will be much better.

<u>Stop and Consider:</u> What are the most important qualities you look for in a partner?

What if you thought you were compatible, went ahead and dove into a serious relationship, and then decided that you're not compatible? Your first job is to examine what happened and whether it's a question of compatibility or something else. Love can blind you, so analyze the situation. Did you just not see the compatibility issues, or did something change? Of course, a change in either one of you or in the relationship could lessen your love to the point that any differences in compatibility could have more impact.

The bottom line to all this discussion about compatibility is that at some point you need to make a decision. Could you decide that the two of you aren't compatible and choose to remain together anyway? Of course you could. Look at all your older relatives, and I'm sure you'll spot a couple or two who aren't compatible but stuck it out. And they may not regret that decision, because there's something to be said for consistency, too.

> **Dr. Ruth Westheimer**
> @AskDrRuth
>
> Being incompatible doesn't necessarily mean you have to split up.

Two people become a couple and stay a couple for an array of reasons. One may be that you form a team that helps both of you cope with life. For example, say you have compatibility issues, but then your mother gets extremely sick and your wife jumps in to help take care of her. How much are your wife's actions worth when deciding whether to stay or go? Imagine a different scenario: compatibility issues lead you to divorce wife number one, and you remarry, this time to someone who is more compatible. Then your mother falls ill again. Your new wife barely knows her, and what she's seen has been mostly a sickly and cranky elderly woman. Will this new wife help her mother-in-law? Probably not. Those ties that bind you to your first wife during all the crucial years you spent together are valuable. Are they enough to keep you together? Maybe not by themselves, but as part of a whole package, they might be the so-called icing on the cake, such that, in hindsight, your first wife's dedication to family might have been important enough to override certain compatibility issues.

As time goes by, this team you created forms many bonds. Or at least it should. I might even say that those bonds are more important to the relationship than the three factors of love, lust, and compatibility I've been discussing. These bonds never would have formed without those three factors being present in the first place. Furthermore, those bonds could end up being strong enough to help you make the decision to stay together.

Having children together is probably the most important factor in forming bonds. As parents, you form a team and go through a lot together. (Of course, if only one of you handles the parenting duties, then maybe instead of creating a bond, parenting duties drive a wedge between you.) Going through a health crisis of some sort can also form a bond, as can helping each other get an education, starting a business, buying and setting up a house, making friends, volunteering at a religious institution or for a political party, taking trips together, and more. These bonds may not be enough to hold you together if there is zero love, zero lust, and zero compatibility, but if the love, lust, and compatibility have decreased, the bonds might be strong enough that your decision is to stay rather than go.

What are these bonds composed of? Your shared memories are the biggest building blocks. Couples remember the birth of their first child, each important moment in their child's development, family vacations, and more. You want to be able to share the experience with someone who was there with you. Shared memories are just more satisfying.

In addition to memories, you've also experienced a whole range of intense emotions, like joy, surprise, anxiety, and pain. Your partner being with you when your mother got cancer and sticking by your side right through the funeral created a bond. Having someone next to you during a crisis does make the crisis easier to bear—and it creates a bond.

Stop and Consider: What bonds exist between you and your partner?

Bonds become stronger over time, or at least they should. As your years together add up, the shared experience grows stronger, because when you replay those memories, your partner is always there by your side. In fact, you might even give your partner a larger role than he or she deserves, because all your shared memories get a bit jumbled. If you've been together for a short amount of time, say three years, you probably don't have as many strong bonds as you would if you were together for thirty years. The longer you're together, the more emotional ties and bonds you'll have.

Bonds are about the past, not the future. If you're not getting along, you're not likely to forge new bonds. But they do have value, so you can't discount them. If love, lust, and compatibility are all gone, bonds are unlikely to make up for their loss. But if these factors are low, then bonds could become a major part of your decision of whether to go or stay.

You can't really analyze bonds created by shared experiences. They're a permanent part of your history. Picture one of those scales with two metal plates on either side of a balanced bar. The bonds are on the plate marked "Stay." Because you can't change history, they're going to be a factor in your decision. But they are what they are, unlike the other three (love, lust, and compatibility), which can change, even on a dime.

Knowing that you're creating bonds might be one reason to make the decision to leave before too many pile up. Bonds are worth their weight, if not in gold, then in life forces. You want to have lots of bonds, because they can help carry you through hard times. But maybe you don't want to accumulate them with the person you're with now. You don't want to waste time with someone who isn't going to be a long-lasting partner. If you think about bonds as the little building blocks that are a part of your life, it might make it easier for you to understand the advantage of leaving sooner rather than later. Picture the bonds you've made as a different color for each important person in your life. The bonds you have with your family are part of your foundation. When you look back on the actual structure of your life, you don't want to see it littered with small batches of different-colored bonds you made with this or that lover who is now somewhere in your past instead of your present.

Dr. Ruth Westheimer
@AskDrRuth

The more bonds you have with one person, the more valuable the pile of bonds becomes.

In pondering the stay-or-go decision, how much importance should you give to what you'll think of your life when you're old and gray and look back on the people you spent time with? Is that viewpoint relevant to your current situation? It is to this extent: if you don't believe that when you reflect later in life your relationship will be something that stands out in terms of reward and joy, then don't hold on to it for flimsy reasons, such as not wanting to be alone on the next Valentine's Day. By taking the long view and considering how you'll feel about your entire life, you might find it easier to decide what your next step might be, whether it be cutting your ties or trying to make repairs.

Stop and Consider: Pretend that you're much older and looking back on your life. Will you enjoy the view?

3.

Let's Communicate About Communicating

Communications are changing so quickly that nobody knows how to communicate anymore, and I include myself in that group. You may be an expert at using your thumbs on your smartphone, but you don't know the long-term consequences of these new ways of communicating. Consider this example. People used to write letters. Writing a letter isn't an instantaneous process, and because letter writers reread what they wrote before sending a letter, maybe over and over, the writer carefully thinks out what to include. On the other hand, text messages take just seconds to compose and send, and they arrive instantly so that they can start a chain of back-and-forth communication that happens so quickly that you barely have a moment to think.

When choosing which restaurant to meet at in a few hours, texting is far superior to letter writing. But when communicating serious issues, texting has far too many deficiencies, not the least of which is you might well regret what you said moments after hitting "Send." The same can happen while talking, but when you are face-to-face, you get feedback from body language, facial expressions, and tone of voice. If your words are hurtful, you're likely to see it. Then you have the opportunity to clarify what you said, soften it, and/or apologize immediately. When talking, your body language actually affects your words. If you have a frown on your face, the same words will seem harsher than if you have a smile. If you raise your voice, the meaning is much different than if you whisper the same words. (Yes, emoticons can help in your texts, but they're not the same.)

Before you send any texts to your partner, analyze them. If the subject matter is serious or could have damaging consequences, then even if you use texting to communicate, write it out first on paper, stop, and think about what you're saying, and only when you're sure you see the ramifications of the content, take out your phone.

> **Dr. Ruth Westheimer**
> @AskDrRuth
>
> Taking a deep breath before texting can save you a lot of grief later on.

Another detrimental aspect of electronic communication is that people are forgetting how to talk to each other. I see so many couples walking down the street or sitting at a restaurant while they're both on their smartphones, not even looking at each other. Check for yourself. Take fifteen minutes to watch people in public. Many of them are on their phones.

Talking is called the art of conversation for a reason. You don't become an artist without practicing your art and concentrating on it. If two people can't hold each other's attention for as long as it takes to eat a meal at a restaurant, don't you think that will have a negative effect when they're talking about a serious issue with their relationship? If your mind is constantly wandering, you can't possibly soak up all the nuances that take place during an important conversation. Words are just one part of a conversation; there are also facial expressions, gestures, tone, and body language, and they're all coming at you simultaneously. If you have something important to say, you may not be able to say everything in words. You may rely on the other aspects of conversation to fully communicate. If the other person is paying attention with only part of his or her brain, at least part of the message is sure to get lost. And if you both have a short attention span, then who knows how much is going to be understood?

Dr. Ruth Westheimer
@AskDrRuth

More than words make up interpersonal communication, so you have to pay close attention.

Because people use more than words when they communicate, you need to practice having real conversations—lengthy discussions without interruption. Multitasking is well and good, but it's not always desirable. It's the epitome of a double-edged sword. Yes, with multitasking, you can fit more into every hour, but the quality of the tasks you're performing isn't as good. So are you really being more productive? When it comes to communicating with your partner, my advice is to concentrate on the task at hand.

Another aspect of not paying attention is that if you and your partner are experts at multitasking, then when you do have a serious conversation, being able to discern whether your true meaning got across becomes more difficult. Was he or she really listening? What if you wanted to be subtle about what you wanted to say? Did your partner understand the message, or was half of it left out in the ether?

Some topics are more difficult to discuss. Allow me to use my specialty, sex, for this example, although the challenges aren't limited to sex. Say that you want to talk about using a new sexual position, perhaps a delicate one like anal sex. Although anal sex has become more common, a man who wants to try anal sex might worry that his female partner will wonder if he has gay tendencies. He might practice raising the topic and asking without being too emphatic with his request. He might want to leave the back door open (pun intended!). Because talking about sexual topics can often be difficult, his facial expressions will be a key in communicating to his partner that he wants to try it, but it's not that important and he'll understand if she turns him down. But what if she's glancing over at her phone while he's saying this, not necessarily picking it up but just wondering whether she might be missing a tweet or Facebook post from someone she follows?

<u>Stop and Consider:</u> Do you give your full attention to your partner when he or she speaks, or are you easily distracted?

A natural response to a situation like this is for the person who was half listening to realize that maybe she missed something important and blurt out "What did you say?" with a concerned look on her face. The conversation instantaneously turns into an uh-oh moment. Now this suggestion, which he wanted to make gently, has landed with a loud thud. Both parties are going to be thrown a little off balance, and the result could go in several directions, a few of which could be damaging to the relationship.

Although I chose a sexual situation as an example, couples have to tenderly handle many other subjects: mothers-in-law (even if you're not actually married). Finances. Household chores. Any topic that once led to a fight, even if you didn't intend it to. Bringing up a topic that is somewhat touchy can be made less dangerous by putting on a smile, but if the partner doesn't see that smile because he or she is texting or e-mailing, then the conversation can turn into a fight. When both parties are under the spell of an adrenaline rush, very little gets communicated.

This leads to my most important tip about communication between partners: practice, practice, and practice some more. Set aside times when you have no distractions, and talk, even if the subject matter is light and breezy. Remember you're having these powwows to improve the communication between the two of you, to learn each other's body language, to pick up subtle references, and to get to know each other better.

Another reason to have these regular conversations is to give you the opportunity to subtly introduce some delicate topic. Saying to a lover, or actually to anyone, "I need to talk to you about something" means that you have something serious to discuss. The stakes have suddenly risen, and the other party might get on the defensive before you've said a word. But if you have scheduled times to talk, then you can bring up any subject in a much lighter spirit. It doesn't have to be the first item up for discussion, and if, while you're talking about something lighter, you notice that your partner's mood isn't suited to a more serious issue, you can postpone the matter until your next scheduled sit-down, when hopefully he or she will be more receptive.

If you think your partner might need some time to digest what you have said, then raise it at the end of your scheduled talk. Just say, "Next time I'd like to talk about such and such, so please think about it." Again, doing that is easier if you have these meetings prearranged.

Some of you are saying at this point, "Dr. Ruth, come on, scheduling times to talk, who does that?" If you're in a good relationship with plenty of opportunities to talk and you make good use of them, this advice clearly isn't pertinent. However, because you're reading this book, you're probably sitting on a fence, wondering about the state of your relationship. The odds are that the communication between you and your lover isn't in the best of shape, so scheduled conversations may be exactly what you need to make progress.

Stop and Consider: How good is the communication with your partner?

When a couple comes to my office, I briefly talk with them together before talking with each of them individually. Without a doubt, I get a different picture of what's going on from each party. Even if they've been talking to each other for hours, they haven't been absorbing what the other person is saying. They've been looking at the situation, whatever it is, from their own perspective, coming up with their own interpretation of the same shared moment. When a couple is in trouble, more than likely their communication needs repair. The same advice I give them applies to you, too: schedule time for some serious conversation with your partner, because you two probably need it.

Be aware that there are good times to talk and bad times. (And because bad times can arise unexpectedly, often because of work-related issues, you have to be flexible when rescheduling your time to communicate.) However, don't make assumptions about what may be an opportune or inopportune moment. Many people would say that they'd prefer not to have a serious conversation at dinner or right after they get home from work, because they need to unwind. Others might say that they'd rather do it when they first get home, because talking helps them forget about the day and, as such, is a way of relaxing. Or they might say that having a discussion too close to bedtime interferes with being able to fall asleep, so the earlier the better. Your first conversation will have to be about when to schedule your conversations so they'll meet both your needs.

Some couples have plenty of opportunities to talk and do so regularly. Or at least they think they do. If you fall into this group, why not keep a diary of how much you talk during one week. If you have breakfast together but are both reading the paper, that doesn't count. If you commute together but have little privacy because you're on a train or a bus, or in a car pool, then that doesn't count either. You would still need to schedule some time for serious topics that you wouldn't want others to hear.

What if you always have music playing, as is common in many households? Music playing in the background might not make a difference, but it might. Here's my suggestion: notice how much you talk and the quality of those conversations, then schedule a date to talk without any background noise and see if you notice a difference. If you don't, then there's no reason to turn off the music. But if communication is better without the music, then you know what you have to do.

An important part of conversation is the question. There are the general questions like "How was your day?" They're important because they show that you're interested in what your partner is doing and what he or she has to say. If you always get a one-word answer like "Fine," then you have a problem that needs to be explored, because each day is different. Something must have happened, so you need to understand why your partner isn't giving you more details. If you're away from each other for ten hours or more every day, "Fine" isn't going to bring you closer together.

"Fine" is an answer often used to dodge a question. There are many other such answers, and it's OK to use short answers when you're rushed or tired or even in a bad mood. However, short answers can't be the only form of communication. If your partner is mostly unwilling to share his or her life with you, then maybe you don't belong under the same roof.

There has long been the notion of a male being the strong, silent type. Perhaps it made some sense back in the days when a man might have been alone with his horse for days or even weeks. In today's world, this behavior just isn't acceptable. When most women were housewives, dependent on their husbands for their financial support, they might have had to put up with someone who never spoke more than a couple of words to them, but today most women aren't locked into accepting such behavior. (Of course, that may not be the case if young children are at home.) The typical woman, especially as depicted in sitcoms, has been represented as a nonstop talker whose husband never listens.

Whatever remnants of these stereotypes still exist must be eradicated. Men and women aren't identical, and they don't have to be. For a romantic relationship to work, it must have shared communication that includes a regular exchange of ideas. Without them, you might as well be roommates.

And then there's that key phrase, "I love you." Some people agonize over when to finally say it. Other people don't worry about whether there is any actual real love behind those words as long as they get what they want.

Of course, love can be communicated in a variety of different ways. I've been known to say that a father changing diapers is a form of foreplay because his actions are clearly showing that by taking on this task he loves not only his baby but also the child's mother. The words "I love you" without the accompanying deeds aren't worth much, and yet the words are important as well.

Every couple deals with stating love as best they can, and its real importance, given the subject of this book, is that if there are no demonstrations of love between two people, there is no actual love. If one half of a couple never wants to hold hands, never wants to cuddle, won't lift a finger to assist his or her partner in any way, forgets every important date, or barely says two words over dinner, then I say that person is saying loud and clear that he or she doesn't have any love in his or her heart.

It is relatively easy for a person to lie. Saying "I love you" takes little or no effort. However, demonstrating love requires involvement, participation, and action. If your relationship doesn't have any involvement, participation, and action, then you can assume it also has very little love. Conversely, if a partner shows his or her love in a variety of physical ways—asking if you want something from the kitchen, doing household chores without prodding, buying little gifts when they're not expected, et cetera—then the words "I love you" become less important. They're nice to hear, but they become the icing on the cake when a person's love is demonstrated regularly.

Stop and Consider: Does your partner demonstrate his or her love?

Don't be shy. If you need to hear the words "I love you" from your partner at least once in a while, and they never say them, though you're sure from their actions that love is in their heart, then speak up. You can ask, "Do you love me?" or you can say, "I need to hear you say that you love me, so please say those words now and again." Some people are better at expressing emotions than others. Your partner may have a heart filled with love for you but get tongue-tied whenever trying to express it. Any encouragement you can give in such a situation will be welcomed by both of you.

> **Dr. Ruth Westheimer**
> @AskDrRuth
>
> Hearing the words "I love you" can be important.

Honesty is one element of good communication that is held in high regard, but I don't believe in always being 100 percent honest. Whether a lie is white or not comes down to intent. Is an honest answer merely frank, or is it mean? In my opinion, if it's mean, then it's better to offer up a white lie. If someone asks, "Does this dress make me look fat?" the answer should never be, "Yes, because you are fat, every dress makes you look fat." That shouldn't be the answer from someone who professes to love you. If the dress isn't the problem, with regards to highlighting size, then saying "You look good in that dress" would be fine. On the other hand, if the dress is part of the problem, then a positive suggestion such as "I like the black dress better" would be appropriate. Fishing for compliments is a risky activity, but I contend that white lies can be useful in keeping a relationship together.

When you observe women in conversation, the norm seems to be to offer up a compliment. If one woman greets another, even if she thinks the other woman's outfit is atrocious, she'll look for the one thing she likes about it and say something like "I really love those earrings." Men, on the other hand, will often do the exact opposite, looking to point out any possible weak point in the other man: "I didn't know that Jason gave haircuts. What's it like to have your hair cut with a chain saw?" Of course, men know that they can't make a similar comment to a woman, but they're better at giving out a quip, which they practice, than they are at giving compliments. Often, they'll say nothing rather than risk saying the wrong thing.

This is an example of the traps that are out there when learning the art of conversation. If you rarely talk about serious matters, then when you do have such a conversation, the mannerisms you've developed when talking to each other—like treating everything as a joke—might lead you astray. Just having a conversation isn't important. What's important is that you're communicating about serious subjects in your relationship. If you're talking at each other instead of listening to each other and engaging back and forth, then any attempt at conversation could be a waste of time.

Another major obstacle to good communication is defensiveness, which is a two-sided coin, because on some occasions, you react defensively, and other times you're putting your partner on the defensive. Words matter, and how you phrase your questions and the points you make are important. You don't want to trigger a fight, because that will lead to less communication, not more. Fighting might be an appropriate response at certain times, but not when you're trying to communicate.

Consider this concrete example. You feel that you're taking on too many of the household chores, yet you both work outside the home the same number of hours. If you start a conversation by stating this fact, your partner is likely to get defensive. The conversation, instead of being productive, will stray into nitpicking, and you'll list each thing your partner has done in the last month and how long it took. You probably won't generate a solution out of such a conversation, because of the defensive reaction you'll likely provoke, especially if your partner feels at all guilty for not doing his or her fair share.

You can start this same conversation by saying, "I'm overwhelmed and need help. Would you mind doing the laundry?" If your relationship is a good one, you'll probably get the help you need. And after the laundry is done, you could ask if this is a chore your partner would be willing to take on permanently. By making concrete suggestions in a way that won't lead to a defensive reaction, you're much more likely to get the results you want.

> **Dr. Ruth Westheimer**
> @AskDrRuth
>
> Phrase your questions so that they don't automatically get a defensive response.

If you want to phrase your questions so they don't get a defensive response, it will take some planning. You have to decide which chore you want to hand off, as opposed to making it an open-ended question. Getting a yes or no answer is a lot simpler than haggling over which chore your partner will take on. Of course, this doesn't mean that your partner might not make a counteroffer. If he or she does, at least you're starting off in a limited fashion that's more likely to yield positive results.

The key is that you take some control over the process. You can't just say, "I want you to do the laundry," and you also don't want to enter extended negotiations. If you prepare defined requests, you're more likely to meet with success. Again, it's the art of conversation. You need to be prepared to excel at it, or at least make use of it to propel your relationship forward. If you never have serious discussions about relationship issues, either because one or both of you avoids them or because you end up fighting, then the quality of your relationship will continue to spiral downward. The bonds of a relationship are dependent on good communication. If your relationship doesn't have those bonds, then it's bound to suffer.

If you want to see proof of the importance of good communication, look at the way some couples manage long-distance relationships. When both partners make an effort to remain in touch, their relationship can stay healthy for extended periods of time. No doubt that people in long-distance relationships have a better understanding of how important it is to stay in touch. If they can do it, certainly a couple who either live together or at least see each other regularly also should be able to do so.

Another stumbling block to effective communication is when you push each other's buttons. You may do this consciously or subconsciously, but either way, elevating the emotional level of a conversation isn't likely to be productive. For instance, say that he knows that he should get a better-paying job, but he hasn't been able to find one. You start a conversation about your next vacation, and he says something about the cost. Having to constantly worry about money irritates you, so for the umpteenth time you throw his salary in his face. There goes that civil conversation. If you want to encourage him to find a new job, that's fine, but that should be part of a separate conversation. If you want to talk about taking a vacation, then you should realize beforehand that cost is going to be a factor that he's going to bring up. If, as you see it, his inability to find a better-paying job has been going on for too long and you're tired of living like a pauper, start making plans to find your next partner. What you shouldn't do is stay in the relationship and cause discomfort by constantly bringing up his low salary. If you love him, want to stay together, *and* want to plan a vacation, give yourself a pep talk before starting this subject so that you're prepared to avoid the topic of his salary. As you can see, conversation is an art that needs practice.

"Come on, Dr. Ruth," you say. "Do I have to worry about what I'm going to say during every conversation with my boyfriend?" No, I didn't say that. But you want him to be thoughtful about the things you care about, so you must show him the same consideration. Men's egos are tied to their jobs. If his job is in a delicate state, tread carefully around that subject, or expect a less-than-positive reaction if you're careless.

<u>Stop and Consider:</u> Are you in the habit of pushing your partner's buttons?

You might be faced with irrationality. Your partner takes off on a tangent that makes no sense. His or her emotions take over, and logic evaporates from the discussion. When that happens, you need a cooling-off period. You have to end the discussion and hope that after some time has elapsed, the two of you can resume an actual conversation with an exchange of ideas. You can't have an effective conversation when one party has stopped making sense.

And never forget, you can hurt someone with words, possibly more than with fists, so don't treat words carelessly. Saying "Oops, I didn't mean what I said to come out that way" isn't an excuse. If you'd thought out what you were going to say before you said it, you might have taken a different approach. Perhaps you meant to use this conversation as one more opportunity to vent your feelings. Doing so is your decision, but the resulting damage to your relationship also becomes your responsibility.

Remember you have to decide whether you want this relationship to go forward, and if the answer is yes, then be careful about how you speak to your partner. If your decision is nearing the "let's end it" line in the sand, starting needless arguments hurts you as much as it does your partner. It's better to just say goodbye than to trigger fight after fight that leaves both of you emotionally drained. If you're not capable of stopping yourself from picking fights with your partner, then move on. And if your partner is constantly picking needless fights with you, the same advice applies.

You're probably familiar with the concept of a "canary in a coal mine": miners take a canary down with them into the mines to judge the air safety. The canary is very susceptible to any poisonous gases, so if the miners see that the canary has died, they know they are in danger of being poisoned and have to leave immediately. Your conversations can be a little like those canaries. If every serious conversation ends up in a fight, then there's a good chance that your relationship is poisonous.

Stop and Consider: Does every conversation turn into a brawl?

When you think of communicating, you usually picture talking or writing to the other person, but people can communicate in many other ways. Touching is an important communication tool, especially between lovers. Looking in each other's eyes is another. How much of your communication includes touching and looking into each other's eyes? The more your relationship is leaning toward the toxic side, the less other forms of communication are probably taking place, so their absence serves as an indication to pay attention.

Stop and Consider: How much touching and looking into each other's eyes is taking place between the two of you?

Another form of communication shows up when you work together at some activity. It's a form of communication that teammates feel when they play a sport, sensing where the other players are and what they're doing, because they know each other so well. When that team spirit isn't there, when one player is hogging the ball, then, more often than not, the team loses the game. If the two of you can cook a meal together, assemble a piece of IKEA furniture, or complete the Sunday crossword without fighting, then that's a positive sign for your relationship. But if you rarely act as a team, or you can't, if the links to even these nonverbal forms of communication are broken, then you do have a problem.

If you don't act as a team very often, look for projects that allow you to build your team. This is especially important because men tend to be attuned to the importance of teamwork and view it as an indication of solidarity. This type of communication isn't a substitute for talking, but if you don't want to part company, looking for other avenues to connect might be crucial to staying together.

With everyone's busy lives, finding the time to have a serious conversation can be hard, and brief electronic messages can't close that gap. If you have something that you need to get off your chest, then make sure that you do. The results will be far better if you've been prepping for this conversation over a period by scheduling talks, shutting down music and other distractions to let your partner know that the conversation is serious, planning what you're going to say and how you're going to say it, and paying attention so that if the situation isn't right for a certain discussion, you're able to postpone it.

4.

Expectations

Your parents set a certain bar in regard to your expectations of a relationship. They could have set it very high or very low, but their relationship is always going to be an important reference point. If they divorced, you'll look at how they behaved, and you'll want to make sure that your relationship is different. If they've been devoted to each other since high school, that will be another model to follow.

Stop and Consider: What is/was your parents' relationship like? How might it be affecting your relationship?

The effects of your family life go far beyond witnessing the relationship that your parents had. How your parents treated you forms part of your psychological makeup. There are other factors, too: Were you an only child? The eldest, middle, or youngest child? What was your relationship with your siblings? Did your grandparents play an important part in your life? What about aunts and uncles?

The years you spent living in the bosom of your family shaped you in many ways. Whether consciously or unconsciously, you may be seeking to re-create that family or run away from it, but the impact your family has had on you may be placing a burden on your partner, who has no idea why you expect him or her to act in a certain way.

<u>Stop and Consider:</u> Are you disappointed in your partner because he or she doesn't fit neatly into your family's behavioral patterns?

Your family relationships are a clear example of what forms your expectations, but what else might influence you? TV and movies are big influences, because you've been absorbing these story lines since you were little. But media is scripted, hence manipulated. Your life isn't. You don't have any control over what's playing on the screen, but you do have a great deal of control over your life, and you have to be able to accept that. That may sound weird, but too many people don't accept that control. They get pushed around; some expect to be mistreated. It's as if they're in a movie and the director is telling them where to stand and what to say. And in many cases, that movie resembles a horror flick.

Situations can change, so after you grab control back you can find ways to make improvements and turn your relationship into a wonderful one. When you don't assert yourself at all, you create a vacuum that your partner is going to step into because somebody has to take control. Your partner may not even want that control, but there seems to be no choice, because you've abandoned it.

Here's an example to consider. For whatever reason, you don't like each other's friends. Because of the negative comments your partner has made, you never invite your friends over, but your partner's friends are always around. Is it written anywhere that this is how it must be? Of course not, so assert yourself. Some nights your partner's friends can come over, and some nights your friends are welcome. Maybe they can even be mixed together, but whatever the outcome, it won't occur unless you exert some control. Don't allow yourself to expect the worst; instead, aim as high as you can.

Look at your life together, and see if any aspects of it seem like a bad script. If they do, try to exert some influence to change what's happening. If you're successful, great; if you're not, then that's evidence that maybe you and your partner aren't well suited.

Stop and Consider: Is control in your relationship shared, or does one of you hold the reins?

There's no doubt that the media has an influence on people's thinking. Many years ago, when the main character on the show *Murphy Brown* became a single mother, I was very angry. Why? Because I knew that a lot of young women would look at that character, see that she was managing her life as a single mom well enough, and conclude that they could copy her, that being a single mom was no big deal. But in real life, being a single mom is rough. I know because I was one. And when you run into trouble, no scriptwriter is there to save the day and give you a happy ending.

Many of today's shows fall into the category of reality TV. Even though the show doesn't have a script, that doesn't mean that the show's producers aren't manipulating what you're watching. The problem with these shows is that they allow the audience members to live vicariously through the characters rather than face the reality of their own lives. If your life is going along swimmingly, it may be all right to indulge in some reality TV. However, if you have your own issues to deal with, don't put off dealing with them while you fantasize about what's going to happen on the next episode of some TV show. And even worse, don't start comparing your life to that of someone on a reality TV show. Your expectations should be based on the possible, not the imaginary. If you're prone to that type of thinking, put your TV in storage until you've settled whatever is wrong with your relationship. You're not in need of distractions. What you need to do is to focus on the reality you're living.

Stop and Consider: Do you use the media to escape from your own reality rather than try to fix it?

Earlier I discussed another possible influence on your relationship, which is the effect your friends can have on you. Your friends are important, but if tomorrow you or your partner was offered a fabulous job in a new city, you'd soon be hanging out with a different set of friends. My point is that friends are great, but someone who might be your lifelong partner is more important. Don't allow your friends to put a target on your partner's back. Remember, some of their reactions may be based on their own inner demons, such as jealousy. Your expectation of what your relationship should be is what's important and what counts. The decision to stay or go is one only you can make, so don't accidentally give your friends a vote.

Your friends also can cause jealousy. If you have several friends who seem to be in an ideal marriage, when you compare your relationship to theirs, you may think, *Why can't I have a life like . . . ?* My advice: stop that immediately. You have no idea what these relationships are like on a daily basis. People can be good at hiding their problems, so basing your view of your own life on your view of other people's lives is a mistake. Allowing envy to affect your relationship is a tactic doomed to failure. If you look around, tons of people are richer, smarter, or better looking than you, and so what? Focus on your situation and your relationship. Don't damage your relationship because you're jealous of what others seem to have in their relationships.

In addition to friends, another important group of peers is coworkers. I advise putting distance between your personal life and the people you see at work. You want to be able to do your work without worrying what they're thinking about you. If you're having relationship issues, they're going to intrude on your thoughts more than you want as it is.

Half a dozen people asking you how you're doing during a workday might end up throwing your concentration so far off that it jeopardizes your job.

You have different sets of expectations. The expectations you have for your career may combine with the expectations you have for your relationship, but not so much that you should allow one set to put the other in jeopardy. There's always the risk that you could lose it all, your relationship and your career, so keep some separation between them.

You may feel like I'm pushing the privacy issue too much here, but what I'm really doing is resetting the bar to where it used to be. Historically, individuals who indulged in gossip were looked down upon; in fact, in the Bible gossiping is a sin. Nevertheless, everyone in biblical times knew that gossip found its way around the neighborhood, and no one wanted to be gossiped about. Today with social media, hundreds of people may know more about you than any one gossip could have passed on. Like it or not, this audience affects you and your relationship, so try to keep some control over your private matters. If you want to tell the world about the delicious meal you had last night at the new restaurant that opened around the corner, great. Post pictures of you on your fabulous vacation, sure. But use a careful filter when sharing any really private matters, like how your relationship is going.

When I had an active private practice, I kept my office in a medical center. That way if a friend or relative saw any of my clients going into that building, they'd have no idea whether they were going in to have their eyesight checked, to have a tooth filled, or to talk to me about their sex life. Privacy is to be treasured because after it's gone, you can't get it back. And, because a loss of privacy can make fixing a relationship much harder, the deeper your relationship problems, the more vigilantly you should protect your privacy.

Dr. Ruth Westheimer
@AskDrRuth

Privacy is a valuable asset, so hold on to it as much as possible.

And what about your own expectations? How much are they worth? If your needs aren't being met, at what point do you decide that the time has come to end the relationship? The first question I would ask is how connected you are with your expectations. How much do they influence what you do with your life? For the sake of this discussion, assume that you're married. When you were planning your wedding, you probably had definitive ideas of how you wanted that big day to go and put in a lot of effort to make sure it met your expectations. But did you establish any expectations about what would come later? Did you discuss them with your new spouse? Were you satisfied with the answers, or were you hoping that it would all work out in the end?

The readers of this book are going to fall into two categories: individuals who had a set of specific expectations and individuals who were just hoping for a general happily ever after. I assume that, for the first group, those expectations were important. For example, if you'd invested time, effort, and money into getting a college degree and found a satisfying job that used the skills you'd acquired, you would expect that your spouse would support your career. If your spouse made degrading comments about your chosen field and maintained that his or her job was more important than yours and that you should make sacrifices that your spouse didn't have to make, then you would have a clear picture that something was seriously wrong with the relationship regarding your expectations. You can use that disconnect between your expectations and reality to draw a line in the sand. If your spouse (and this would apply to any partner in a serious relationship) prevents you from moving forward in your chosen career, don't tolerate that behavior.

If you fall into the second group, making a decision may be harder. If you didn't know what marriage would be like but went ahead because you were madly in love with your spouse, you'd be in a position where you'd be more likely to compromise. In that kind of situation, you might be more willing to put your spouse's wishes first, which isn't necessarily bad, because doing so is a personal decision. The choice is up to you. If you don't feel good about the relationship, if your love has diminished or just isn't strong enough to make up for the state of your relationship, then you probably have to go back and examine what those expectations might have been. You have to know what you're giving up before you will be able to decide that it outweighs the relationship.

Stop and Consider: Are you aware of anything you're giving up to stay in your relationship?

My father-in-law didn't attend my wedding to my now ex-husband. He thought we weren't right for each other, so he wasn't going to bless our union with his presence. At the time, I obviously disagreed with him, but I changed my mind. My husband and I had no animosity between us; there just wasn't enough substance to our relationship to make keeping it together a worthwhile proposition. I finally realized—we both did—that his father had been right, and we weren't a good match. We hadn't fully thought out what we would be like as a married couple, and it made more sense not to continue being married.

Your expectations are important, even if you're not aware of them and have to figure them out after the fact. A vague feeling that something is lacking between the two of you isn't enough reason to give up on a relationship. You need to identify concrete issues that aren't working. You need to know what they are so that you can see whether the two of you can fix them. If they are fixable, great; if they aren't, then move on. Taking stock of your expectations is part of the process.

5.

Financial Pressures

Any kind of financial problems will exert pressure on a relationship. If the relationship already has some fractures, then financial pressure can widen the cracks. Understanding the unique ways that financial issues can disrupt your relationship will help you identify them and possibly avoid them.

Men have traditionally been the breadwinners. Their egos usually are closely tied to their jobs, and much of their status is job related. When a man loses his job, especially if he is out of work for a considerable period, it is going to cause him psychological issues. For example, most men in this situation lose some, if not all, of their desire for sex. If you, as a couple, don't know this, when your sex life takes a nosedive, you both might reach the wrong conclusion. A wife might think, *He's home all day, so maybe he's cheating with the neighbor next door.* Or he might think, *She's put on a little bit of weight. I guess I'm not attracted to her anymore.*

If a man's ego is bruised, he might develop a short fuse. His temper might flare up, and neither of you will understand why. As a result, fights can become regular occurrences, and the relationship can face more stress.

I obviously can't help the man in your partnership find a job, which would probably fix such a situation. Understanding the source of any conflicts that develop is important; then, being able to understand that they're not personal and hopefully temporary is also key to maintaining a good relationship. Having this information can help you both to weather the storm. He might still feel depressed, he might still lack a sex drive, he might still blow up over nothing, but comprehending that the underlying reason isn't related directly to your relationship can give you added patience.

Stop and Consider: Could financial pressures be causing your relationship to develop cracks?

When a woman loses her job, she will also face depression and reduced libido, but the symptoms might not be as strong as they are for men. Though today most women do work outside the home, there are still enough women who don't go to an office every day that a woman might not feel as down about her situation. A man who is out of work and doing the grocery shopping midday during the week may feel that everyone is staring at him while thinking, *Loser.* Of course, these days there are a lot of stay-at-home dads, but most of the time they've consciously made that choice. A woman is much less likely to feel so out of place in such situations. She can take comfort in the fact that most people will assume she's a housewife with kids at home to take care of, so her ego isn't so much at stake.

What if you're both working, but you just keep finding yourself running short of money? That situation poses different kinds of pressure, because it's constant. When someone loses a job, he or she always has the hope that a new job is just around the corner. However, when you're both employed and still not bringing home enough to cover expenses, you may be locked into a hopeless situation. Hopeless for you unless, perhaps, you get out of the relationship and find someone new to team up with. I'm not saying that money troubles are a necessary cause of a rupture, but they're likely to cause the possibility of making a change to pop into your brain. If you're wondering why you are stuck in a mess, then you might also start to poke one foot out the door. After that happens, the relationship is going to wind up on shaky ground, even if everything else seems to be going fine.

What you need to remember in such situations is that you're supposed to be a team. What you do together as a team might make a difference. So if one of you needs to go back to school to get a better job, making the sacrifice to live together under an even tighter budget to create change might be worth it.

> **Dr. Ruth Westheimer**
> @AskDrRuth
>
> Financial pressures are better handled as a team.

To operate as a team, you both must be fully informed about your financial situation. If one of you is playing his or her cards close to the vest, keeping the other in the dark about how bad financial matters actually are, then working together toward fixing them is going to be impossible.

If your team isn't playing well together, then making a bigger sacrifice won't seem like a good idea. If such a situation is on the horizon, it's better to make the decision to stay or go before committing to making sacrifices. You certainly wouldn't want to be the person making the sacrifice, working even harder to help pay for a partner's schooling, only to have that partner leave after he or she earned the degree. And if you have a conscience, you wouldn't want to be on the other side of that equation either. You might then feel forced to stay in a relationship that you know deep down isn't the right one for you. (And yes, getting an education does change you; afterward, you might not look at your partner in the same way.)

Another financial decision that can be risky if your relationship isn't going well is signing any sort of agreement that involves borrowed money. What happens if you buy a condo together and a short while later you break up? From a legal standpoint, you still have to pay your share of the loan. However, because you may be living somewhere else, you're paying for two places. Yes, you can eventually sell the condo, but if your former partner isn't being cooperative, selling it might take months or even longer, depending on the real-estate market. Before signing any such papers, make sure that your relationship is on solid footing. Although the ground can suddenly shift under any relationship, if you see any signs of instability, then don't sign on the dotted line until you've made changes to shore up that foundation.

Stop and Consider: What financial liabilities do you have that are directly related to your relationship?

Some people might feel that making a commitment to something like buying a condo is like making a commitment to the relationship. You could say to yourself, *He's not proposing, but he does want to buy this condo with me, so he must be committed to me.* That line of thinking does have some logic to it, but it's somewhat twisted logic. Ask yourself what would be holding him back from marrying you if he's willing to buy a condo with you. Buying a condo is a business deal. You can do that with anyone, your uncle Charlie for example. You're supposed to be in love, yet he won't take that last step and marry you. Find out why. I say this not because I'm that concerned that you're making a bad financial deal, but rather because you'll end up with a broken heart.

If someone doesn't commit to you, it means there's an emotional vacuum. The danger is that someone else could step in and fill it. He likes you well enough, he likes spending time with you, and he likes having sex with you, but if he's not sure that he really loves you, then don't tie the financial knot before the matrimonial one.

> **Dr. Ruth Westheimer**
> @AskDrRuth
>
> Tie the knot before you make any financial commitments to each other.

Another situation that arises regarding finances is when the two people aren't on the same page about money. That usually means one likes to spend, and the other likes to save. Those differences aren't just around the edges. They're fundamental and maybe even extreme. Of course, you might be the one with the extreme take on spending and thus the source of the conflict between you. The path you take together should be one that will cause the least amount of discord, and that might be to save some money and spend some. If you're the one who either spends every last cent or never spends a cent, then my sympathies are with your partner. Spending the rest of my life with someone like that would also make me think twice. If that's the case, you may need to see whether you can adjust your views on money. But if your partner has an extreme point of view, then it might be serious enough to decide to leave. Just don't drag out the process of making the decision. If your partner's views on money are sufficiently annoying to prevent you from making a commitment, then look for someone more compatible.

As I've said and will continue to say, when you run into a problem about which you can't make up your mind, and you're not sure whether you're having an exaggerated reaction to your partner's behavior, get help. If your finances are shot, then you probably can't afford to get professional help. The answer in such situations is to look for free help. One source could be a religious leader, who won't charge you, has some experience in such matters, and will maintain your privacy. Sometimes just unburdening yourself can relieve some of the pressure. Although I retain my position on talking to friends, if you're strapped, and sometimes even if you're not, talking to older relatives—aunts, uncles, grandparents—can be a source of comfort. They've seen more of life than you have; if you ask them, they're likely to keep these conversations private. That's why they can provide a safe place to unburden at no cost.

6.

Common Interests / Common Conflicts

For the record, I'm a Jew. I would date only Jewish men, because I would want to be married only to a fellow Jew. My religion is sufficiently important to me that it's a make-or-break condition. If you have strong views about religion or politics or anything else, then you should work that into your approach to forming romantic interests and be choosy concerning those interests. That's not to say that people of different religions, political views, races, ethnicities, or cultures can't create strong lifelong bonds. In fact, opposites may attract, and that attraction can be quite strong. However, when two people are on divergent paths, those differences can also cause serious conflicts.

Remember, this book isn't for the in-love couple who want to spend every single second together and who have zero complaints about each other. This book is for the person who's wondering whether to stay or go. Maybe when you first got together your differences weren't important, but they have since become more so; perhaps you've gotten over that "blind" love stage, and the source of irritation was always there but you hadn't yet felt it. Or maybe after a while some aspects of your partner's lifestyle have accumulated to the point where they've gotten on your nerves.

Also, with the passage of time, it's possible your views changed. Some people go through a period during which religion isn't important to them, and then something happens and they return to the flock. When you first met your partner, your religious differences might not have been much of an issue, but they can suddenly become a huge obstacle. Religion can have important consequences when it comes to marriage. Although the civil portion of marriage is necessary from a legal standpoint, the religious portion of the marriage ceremony will likely play a much bigger role on a wedding day, especially because most wedding festivities are held after the religious ceremony and not after a trip to city hall to get a marriage certificate.

The same can be true for any other set of differences, including cultural, political, and social ones. You're entitled to change your mind, but doing so can end up causing a rift with your lover.

The first question to ask yourself is whether this difference in interests is the actual source of any conflict. If not, has something in the relationship changed your feelings about something that you once could ignore but now has become an irritant?

For example, say that your partner is British. In British culture, yes can mean no, because that culture says not to hurt the other person's feelings by rejecting their request, while in America we are more straightforward with our replies. When you were first dating, you might not even have noticed that your partner was agreeing to something and then doing the opposite, so this cultural difference didn't stop you from falling in love and moving in together. Now that you're living under the same roof, not being able to understand the answers to your questions is driving you crazy. This cultural difference could be the main source of conflict, but it also might be something else entirely. For example, what if the two of you like to party on weekends, but when your partner gets drunk he or she turns nasty? You could propose that the two of you stop drinking so much, but then you'd have to stop as well, and you don't want to do that. Instead you place the blame for the gulf that is growing between the two of you on some cultural differences, which may, in fact, exist. The real underlying issue is the personality change your partner undergoes after having had too much to drink.

Stop and Consider: Are any conflicts you have with your partner cultural?

Conflict colors your thinking in many ways. If you're fighting with someone over one issue, more than likely you'll disagree with that person over other issues as well, maybe even in a knee-jerk manner, such as "If he supports that candidate, there must be something wrong with him." When you're in a serious relationship, you need to understand what is really going on. In this example, you can't change your partner's background, and if that is the main problem, then I would tell you to break up. But if something else is going on in your relationship, and the two of you don't yet recognize that you could repair that issue, then your relationship is in needless jeopardy.

Analyzing a relationship is a bit like analyzing a health issue. If you can figure out that the headaches you're suffering from began on a certain date, and that's when they installed new carpeting in your office, you can deduce the fumes from the new carpeting are causing your headaches. When examining your own relationship, you can't just look at its present state, or even what happened the night before, but instead you must look farther back. If you were perfectly happy for two years and then you noticed changes in how you felt about your partner, you need to comb through your past to see whether you can spot an occurrence around that time that might have caused the change. There's no guarantee that you'll discover the source of the problem or that there is just one rather than cumulative disappointments, but searching is well worth it.

Looking back at your relationship may help guide you to where it is headed.

Some people weren't right for each other from the beginning and should never have become a couple. If that's your situation, then you need to go back in time to when you first met and examine the reasons why you're not meant to be a twosome.

Let me be clear: you don't have to be like two peas in a pod to have a wonderful relationship. Two people may love antiques, run an antiques business together, and spend all their days and nights living and breathing antiques. As a result, their relationship profits immensely from all this togetherness. But more likely than not, this isn't your situation; instead, the two of you lead separate lives that intersect at certain points but are disconnected for long stretches of the day. If you're not entirely satisfied with your relationship, I'd recommend developing some common interests, especially if you don't have children.

Children are a natural common interest, and they can be time-consuming, so you have little opportunity for much of anything else. But if you don't have children, young ones anyway, then assuming you don't want to waste your lives just watching a video screen, you need to have outside interests. Boredom is deadly to a relationship (and I'm not talking about boredom in the bedroom), so developing some outside interests is essential, and hopefully one or two interests will appeal to both of you so you can share them.

Staying together when your only common interest is your children is another matter entirely. I don't necessarily agree with that route, and I think divorce is preferable. Children living with parents who are always yelling and screaming at each other may be worse off than children with parents who are no longer married. Children are an important consideration when making the stay-or-go decision, but they tip the scales only a certain amount in favor of staying. When children are involved, you must make every effort to make repairs to the relationship. If the relationship becomes too toxic, then everyone might be better off splitting the family in two, including the children.

Another path you can follow is to take the plunge and become more deeply invested in your partner's interests and culture. If he or she has a significantly different background, you can study the language, learn to appreciate the cuisine, cook in that nation's style, and immerse yourself in the history of that land. The gesture alone will be one your partner should treasure (and if he or she doesn't, then maybe that's a sign that you need to investigate that reaction), and it also will bring you closer together.

If you have different religions, and one or the other of you doesn't convert, you can still learn as much as you can about your loved one's religious beliefs. Doing so would undoubtedly allow you to get a bit closer to his or her family, which is always good for the health of a relationship.

Some advice that I give to singles is appropriate here. I tell singles that they should partake in activities that increase the likelihood of meeting someone, but when doing so, they should choose their activities carefully. For example, if they take a class at a community college that doesn't end up offering the opportunity to meet a partner, at least they should select something that they enjoy. That way they're sure to get a return on their investment. The same philosophy applies to someone in a relationship trying to share a partner's interests. If you've always hated watching sports, trying to follow your partner's team just to be doing something together is likely only to cause resentment. But if your partner likes to run, and so far you have not gotten into running but are willing to try, then training together for an upcoming charity 5K would be a positive activity to share. Choose wisely when making any attempts to draw closer to one another; if you don't choose something you are at least somewhat interested in, you might end up creating more distance instead.

The more effective path to form new bonds with one another might be to start fresh with some activity. Maybe you both have a bucket list, and if you compare them, you'll find some points where they intersect, such as reading *War and Peace*. Maybe you could get the audio version and listen to it together and discuss your thoughts. Or if after the first chapter, you both decide that you've had enough, you can stop. (Don't put the blame on your relationship but on Tolstoy!) You can then return to those bucket lists and choose something different, such as camping or gardening.

What if you can't find common ground? What if your bucket lists are so different that you just don't see an activity that you could share? Does that mean you're not suited? Maybe, but it depends on your personalities. Some people do well on their own. It's not that they don't like being with people, but they also don't mind being solo. Many only children probably are like that. On the other hand, people who come from a large family are more likely to feel comfortable surrounded by other people and will have a strong desire to share activities with the person they love, in part just to be with them. If they can't be with the person they love, they'll gravitate toward others. Long periods of separation could hurt the relationship.

Here's where the concept of opposites attract doesn't necessarily hold up. If two lovers were opposites in that she liked to run marathons and he liked to read long books like *War and Peace*, as long as they also spent time together doing other things, their relationship would be fine. But if she adored an activity that required a partner, like ballroom dancing, and he hated to dance, then there might be a problem. When examining your interests and your compatibility, you really have to delve deeper than merely looking at the interests themselves. Your personalities will cause secondary ramifications that you should take note of to understand. Nothing the two of you do or say is in a vacuum. When deciding whether this is the relationship for you, you must look at the full context to make the right decision.

<u>Stop and Consider:</u> What interests do you share with your partner?

Sometimes your interests inherently cause conflicts. He's a huge sports fan and parks himself in front of the TV all weekend long. You'd love to spend a Sunday afternoon with him at a museum or seeing a matinee, but that's always out of the question because there's always a big game on. Not only does he enjoy watching sports, but also he feels the need to watch so he can talk sports with his father, brother, and friends. He's not willing to give that activity up, even though as far as you're concerned it's significantly weakening your relationship.

You knew he liked sports when you met him, but in the early days of the relationship he made compromises. He'd go bike riding with you on a Sunday afternoon, which, now that you're living together, he refuses to do.

In such situations, you have several options. One extreme, of course, is just to go along to get along. At the other extreme is getting out of the relationship. The middle options would require some compromises. And reaching a compromise usually requires negotiations. To be a successful negotiator, decide how small a compromise you would accept and then ask for more, always considering your bottom line. Starting such a discussion doesn't force you into any position if you don't want it to. You could decide ahead of time that you're not going to leave over this issue, but you should still try to get some movement. If you have a bottom line that requires some compromise from your partner, then you must be ready to act. In this situation, once you start this process, you have to insist on some change occurring. Otherwise, why try at all?

Knowing how good your partner is at negotiating is critical to your success. If your partner senses that giving in even a little might lead to a slippery slope, he or she may take a firm stand against any compromise, which may lead to the end of your relationship. If that's the case, so be it. You're not all that happy with your relationship the way it currently is. If your partner refuses to make any compromises, then your best bet may be to move on.

7.

Couples Politics

When you hear the word "politics," you immediately think of elections, Democrats and Republicans, and public officials. But my concern here is your relationship, and no matter which party you each belong to, the way the two of you react to each other has a political component.

You've certainly heard the term "office politics." This one won't share power, that one is always sucking up to the boss, and the other one will do anything to get out of taking responsibility. These types of interactions also affect just two people, and I like to call this "couples politics."

What differentiates the business world from the political world is that businesses are trying to amass the most money, and politicians are seeking to gather the most power. Every US senator basically makes the same amount of money, but some are much more powerful than others. That power struggle can also take place in your relationship. A certain amount of power is in your possession as a couple, and it's either being shared or being hogged.

The old expression "the man wears the pants in the family" refers to the idea that he's the boss and what he says goes. When being the strongest physically bestowed power, men were the boss, though many women figured out how to grab much of that power, even if the man didn't realize what was happening. These actions by the women could be considered a political move. The women didn't need to be physically strong; they just needed to know how to work within the political system of their society and their marriage.

Today the stereotype of the man being the head of the household is disappearing, though it's not entirely gone. How you each feel about power is going to affect your relationship. (I wrote a book called *Power: The Ultimate Aphrodisiac* that deals mostly with famous powerful people rather than the power struggles that go on within a household.) When making the ultimate stay-or-go decision, you need to examine the politics of your relationship. This may not be easy, because grabs for power aren't always obvious.

In some couples, the man is the more powerful of the two, and both partners are quite happy with that situation. Some justify this on biblical grounds. If both husband and wife agree, then such an arrangement isn't a problem. Usually in these situations, even if the man has the final say, the woman often manages to have her share of power in the long run.

If both partners are quite willing to share the power, this issue isn't a problem. Where relationship problems arise is when there is a power struggle—when one person tries to dominate the other. If you're caught in such a situation, then sometimes the only solution is to head for the exit door. But doing so can be difficult when you feel like you don't have much power. You can feel dominated, and then making the decision to leave can become a heavy burden that you're not sure you can handle.

If you're caught in this type of situation, change your perspective. Yes, leaving might be difficult, even somewhat scary, but in the long run you'll be much better off. Keep your view glued to this new happier future, and you'll find it easier to handle a difficult situation in the present. The worst thing you can do is be miserable in the present while simultaneously believing that the future is hopeless.

How do you decide whether any relationship conflicts you're experiencing are signs of a power struggle? Start with looking at them from that point of view. You might never have thought of doing this kind of analysis on your own. If one of you always has to be right and get his or her way, figure out why. If your partner is always getting his or her own way, ask yourself why your opinions don't matter. If your partner is trying to hog all the power, it doesn't matter how logical you are, because your partner is adamant about not giving up any control at all. It's not the actual subject matter of your discussion but rather the principle of always being the one to decide what's important to your partner. It might even be a cut-off-your-nose-to-spite-your-face situation, but your partner prefers being wrong and maintaining control to admitting to being wrong and ceding some power.

Stop and Consider: Does one of you hold a lot more power than the other, or is it mostly shared?

Often people who need to make others feel weak are covering up their own weaknesses or insecurities. Maybe a parent or older sibling dominated them when they were young, and they've chosen, perhaps unconsciously, to grab as much power as they can so as not to fall into a similar situation. If you find yourself in a situation in which you're living with someone who won't share and who makes you extremely uncomfortable, your only choice is to leave, unless your partner is willing to go to therapy. Reaching a compromise is an unlikely proposition, so your choice becomes either submit or end the relationship.

Some people grab power because experience has taught them the benefits of it, so they go after power whenever they can. It may be an ingrained habit. They don't even realize that their behavior is spoiling their romantic relationship; they might even be willing to cede some power if requested. These people might revert to grabbing power on occasion, but the two of you may be able to reach a successful compromise.

How can you spot power grabs? One common, though relatively unimportant power struggle among couples is over the TV remote. That's a visible one; whoever holds the remote has the power. Clearly this isn't a serious issue, but it can point to bigger problems in areas that don't have such telltale signs. What really counts is the overall pattern. If one person is always getting his or her way and the other person resents it, then that's a serious relationship issue. If you're staring at a future in which you never get to decide anything, even the TV show you'll watch, then maybe that's a future you'd be better off without.

One important ingredient of politics is horse trading. You do this for me, and I'll do this for you. Let me say that I am against threats. I don't want you to ever say, "Either you do such and such, or I'm leaving!" If conditions are that bad between the two of you on a regular basis, then leaving may be the option you want to choose. However, I have nothing against looking ahead to a decision that will need to be made and offering something up in exchange for getting your way. Just do so in a civil manner.

Such an exercise is healthy for a relationship. It forces you to look at your partner in a different light. You have to think about your partner's wants and desires, weigh them against yours, and decide what is acceptable to you and what isn't. Human beings have been trading since time immemorial, but to some extent we have lost that ability. Today you walk into a store, and there's a tag offering you a fixed price and a cashier who doesn't have the power to change it even if you made a different offer. In many stores, you don't even encounter a cashier; the checkout process is automated. But humans need to interact with one another, and learning how to trade, how to discuss a price, and how to remain civil and friendly are important life lessons. If this type of interaction is something you rarely do, that inexperience will make it harder to negotiate with your partner. But after you learn how to trade, you'll be able to do it more easily in everyday life. Remember the key is to come out of the trading session still loving one another. If you can't trade without feeling regret, then go back and hone your trading skills.

Stop and Consider: How good are your trading skills?

If your partner refuses to negotiate and insists on having his or her way, then that's another lesson you'll have learned. If compromise isn't part of your relationship, then your relationship is a damaged one. Damaged enough to cause a split? That decision will depend on many other factors, but it certainly is damaged enough to warrant a serious examination.

If you've never negotiated with your partner, but you can figure out how to do it, that bodes well for the relationship as a whole. It's an avenue for making progress in whatever areas need work.

Stop and Consider: Do you and your partner have successful negotiations, or is one of you always right?

Politics can also teach you to take matters less personally. I get so many questions from people who insert their emotions into a partner's actions when there's no actual reason to do so. For example, as men get older, they lose their ability to get an erection from outside stimuli like the sight of a naked woman and require actual physical stimulation. In other words, at a certain age, men need foreplay just the way women do. If a man undergoing this change has a wife who doesn't know about this natural occurrence, she might jump to the conclusion that he no longer finds her attractive, perhaps because she gained a few pounds. The fact that he no longer automatically gets an erection when he sees her naked has nothing to do with her; he's undergoing a physical change. In other words, don't automatically take things personally and jump to conclusions.

In the case of the loss of psychogenic erections (the technical term for an erection caused without physical sensation), the misunderstanding between husband and wife can increase by leaps and bounds. She may think he's no longer becoming aroused by her body because he's having an affair with his new employee, which can start a chain reaction that leads to a split. If he doesn't understand what is happening to his body, he could jump to the wrong conclusion as well, believing that his wife no longer appeals to him, so he may start an affair with a coworker.

Certainly, a slight can be personal. If one spouse is sent to buy a birthday cake and comes back with a strawberry shortcake knowing that the other spouse is allergic to strawberries, that's cause for being upset. However, in general don't jump to conclusions, because doing so just makes some situations a lot harder to negotiate.

> **Dr. Ruth Westheimer**
> @AskDrRuth
>
> Don't jump to conclusions until you have all the evidence.

For a political system to work, both sides have to communicate. If the two of you stop talking because of some argument over a small matter, the split can grow larger and larger until a small slight has grown into an all-out war. What you have to do when there's a fight is get back to that negotiating table. You must explain to one another what you were thinking and be willing to forgive and forget. You both have an interest in your relationship working, so it's important to learn how to manage your emotions so that it can.

Failing to come to a compromise after a fight is a bad sign. The reason may have nothing to do with what you were fighting about; more than likely an underlying problem in your relationship—a problem that needs to be fixed if the relationship is to continue—is causing the fight to linger.

In an Italian form of theater called commedia dell'arte, the male actors playing women wore masks. Italians even today will don figurative masks, exaggerating the intensity of their emotions so that during a fight, a little bit of anger seems to grow to a boiling pot, though in actuality it's just mask. If such exaggeration is part of your culture, then cultural norms are also in place to allow everything to go back to normal. But for most people, when you're arguing with your spouse and you don a mask of outrage that you don't really feel, it's likely to be interpreted as real anger, which is especially true if your relationship is a little ragged. You must learn to turn the temperature of your arguments down, not up.

No matter what your cultural background is, your attitude toward fighting is likely to have been formed in large part by the fights you witnessed between family members, particularly your parents, when you were growing up. If there was a lot of screaming and yelling, then that's going to be your natural reaction. If it was the norm for your mother to walk away and lock herself in her room, then you might do the same to avoid a knock-down, drag-out fight. In one family, cursing might have been standard during a fight, while in another family, the parents would never curse, especially in front of the children. (Some parents never fight in front of the children, leaving them to guess how best to handle such conflicts when they become adults.)

If you and your partner come from families that had very dissimilar ways of fighting, then your reactions to arguments are going to be quite different. One of you may be used to raising his or her voice, because that was the norm, but a raised voice might be shocking to the other person, causing him or her to burst into tears rather than scream back. Leaving the scene of an argument when it's barely begun can prove frustrating to a partner used to fully hashing out an argument.

At some quiet moment, I urge you and your partner to talk about your inherited fighting styles. Ask each other how your family fought, what the rules were, and how everyone behaved. Every couple fights now and then, and understanding your partner's reactions is important to keeping the level of miscommunication to a minimum.

Stop and Consider: Have you and your partner discussed what behavior is appropriate when you fight?

It's better not to argue too vehemently in the first place. If you find that an argument is getting heated, call a time-out, go back to your corners, think about how you really feel, and then try to settle the matter more civilly. Easier said than done? Perhaps. But if your relationship is valuable to you, then you have to be willing to put in the effort. Remember that effort can take a couple of forms: not doing something or doing something else.

> **Dr. Ruth Westheimer**
> @AskDrRuth
>
> Not doing something can be as important as doing something else.

If one partner has a short fuse and disagreements are always turning into fights, professional anger management may be appropriate. If you're constantly the victim of these outbursts, you may have to start considering an exit strategy. What you don't want is to be verbally beaten; it will take a toll on your life, and you don't want to let that go on for too long.

If you're reacting strongly to any possible disagreements and cringing before any nasty words have been thrown your way, you're in a relationship that needs to end. Your psychological makeup is being changed, you're becoming conditioned to expect an angry outburst, and that's not a way to live the rest of your life. If your partner is willing to go for help, you can wait to see if it works, but if not, then take immediate action.

Stop and Consider: **Do you cringe before an argument has even begun?**

Humans are political animals and can react in certain ways based on beliefs, just like those individuals who belong to one political party or the other. However, in a couple, you're supposed to be lovers, and lovers make sacrifices for their beloved. Being able to spot when the politics of your relationship are making you act as an opponent instead of a lover is important. If you can't make that leap back to being a lover, then maybe your next move will be out of the relationship.

8.

When Your Job Gets in the Way

Modern societies haven't fully adapted to the concept of women who work outside the home. Different countries have adopted an assortment of rules concerning maternity leave, and the United States not only falls behind many of these nations but also fails to ensure that women are paid as much as men (not to mention the glass ceiling when it comes to rising to the top). Society is changing, and I hope eventually women won't be treated as second-class citizens, but for now, couples must adapt to the current reality, which remains in flux. Without adequate cultural norms to fall back on, couples are forced to invent their own rules, which often can lead to confusion that puts a strain on the relationship.

Because there are no absolute rules, couples are free to adapt any way they agree. If a woman who works a job that is just as all-consuming as her spouse's still gets stuck doing most of the housework yet is willing to put up with that situation, no one is forcing her to stay. Not what you expected to hear? I'm not saying that situation is good. What I am saying, and have been saying again and again, is that if you find yourself in this same situation, you shouldn't allow peer pressure—from family, friends, or society in general—to force your hand one way or the other. If your friend says, "You mean you do all the cleaning and cooking? That's outrageous!" just tell her to mind her own business. If you love your husband and you feel that you get so much out of the relationship that doing this extra work is worth it, that's your decision. And the same goes for a man who has to turn down his friend's offer to go to a game because he has to do laundry. Only you can decide what the right decision is for you.

However, you do need to decide. If you're stuck in an unfair situation and aren't happy about it and you don't want to accept it and feel frustrated by it, then start thinking about whether it's time to get out of it. Remember that there are no ground rules anymore. Women used to stay home while men went to work, but those days are long gone. You have to examine your role in your relationship to decide whether it's fair or not. If it's unfair, determine whether it's so unfair that it's worth breaking up over. (Again, only you get to decide whether it's fair; only your reaction counts.)

I know some feminists are going to disagree with me and would tell a woman that she must demand that her partner take an equal role when it comes to housework. My position of not being so adamant on this point comes, in part, from being a sex therapist. Women, in general, take longer than men to have an orgasm, and I say that a man needs to spend whatever time his partner requires to give her sexual satisfaction. Which situation would be less fair, that he has to put in more time and effort than he requires for sexual satisfaction or that she not have an orgasm? I hope that when thinking about this question you conclude that sometimes fair has nothing to do with these matters. I'm not saying you should put up with an unfair situation, but I am saying that your decision shouldn't be imposed on you by any outside influences. It is also possible that your love for your partner might tempt you to accept an unfair situation.

Stop and Consider: Is your relationship placing an unfair burden on your time?

This question of unfairness is especially important if the unequal sharing of housework or childcare is jeopardizing your career. If you're too exhausted to put in your best effort at work, if you feel pressured into leaving work early to go home and cook dinner, then you need to weigh those factors. Is this job really important to you? Is it one that will impact the rest of your career in a positive way, assuming that you can meet all the challenges? If you're not fully committed to spending the rest of your life with your partner and he or she is interfering with the career you're invested in, then that could be enough of a reason to leave.

Stop and Consider: Should you put your job ahead of your current relationship?

These situations may be clear-cut, and the decision, although difficult, may be obvious. But what if you're in a gray zone? What if staying and leaving have pros and cons? Because this chapter is about your job, why not think of it in terms of money? If your job is an important step in your lifetime ladder for success and your relationship is keeping you from climbing as high as your potential might allow, figure out how much money it might cost you over the next twenty or more years if you were to lose that job or get passed over for promotion: $100,000, $500,000, or even more? Maybe you can't put a price on love, but if you're having doubts about your love relationship, if it may not last for reasons having nothing to do with your job, then recognizing this potential lost income might be sufficient reason to leave.

Dr. Ruth Westheimer
@AskDrRuth

Money can't buy you love, but that doesn't mean you shouldn't examine the costs of that love.

Again, if you're reading this book because you're just not sure of what to do, putting a dollar amount on whether to stay or go could help simplify that decision for you. Doing so isn't crass; it's practical. You have a decision to make, and your financial interests should be put into the overall equation.

Making sacrifices for true love can pay off in a way that warrants putting it ahead of your career. But if you're not sure that you're going to be in this relationship for all that long, then maybe your career has to come first. Maybe the better outcome for you is going to be a hard break. Lingering in a relationship that's hurting your career isn't a wise move. Other potential partners are out there; you won't be alone for the rest of your life. If you need to make a decision, make it sooner rather than later, or else you might end up losing the relationship and damaging your career.

Your salaries also can impact your relationship. One of you might be following his or her dreams, to be an artist or a writer, for example, but not making much money at it, which forces the other partner to work harder to pay the bills. It's a sacrifice, especially if the person making money doesn't really love his or her job.

As I've said, this is an issue only if you feel it's an issue. If your parents are saying, "Why do you stay married to that bum who doesn't earn a living?" that question needn't influence you. If you love the "bum" and he or she loves you back, then that's all that matters. But if it really annoys you that you're the sole breadwinner, and if you occasionally wonder why you are in this relationship, then stop lingering and decide to go. Or decide to stay, and stop driving yourself crazy with doubts about the relationship.

Some couples work together. Having relationship issues that are severe enough to cause a split is going to cause them a pain in the wallet as well as in their hearts. If that's the case for you, look at the overall situation and see whether working together or spending too much time together is causing your relationship problems. In this type of situation, making a move to separate your careers might allow you to maintain the relationship. How much you love each other doesn't matter. Your relationship can be put under so much stress that it can't possibly hold up, and working together might be one of those stressful situations. You might not have realized it. You might even have thought it would be terrific for the two of you to spend so much time together, but it may not be best for your relationship. Your personality may dictate that you need some more breathing space, and being together 24/7 isn't allowing for that. Or perhaps your partner is dominating when making business decisions. If you joined his existing business, then maybe you need to find employment that allows you more freedom to express yourself. In any case, stop working together and see what happens. Even if the relationship still falls apart, the likely outcome would probably be separate careers, so why not start with that first step?

> **Dr. Ruth Westheimer**
> @AskDrRuth
>
> Working together may seem romantic, but it can also be stifling.

When considering work hours, you also have to account for commuting. A long commute, done twice a day, can be as much of a burden as working a job with long hours, especially if you're both in a situation with long work hours and a long commute. This is one more issue to weigh. Ask yourself some important questions: Why do you live so far from where you work? Is it entirely your decision, or is your partner benefiting in some way that causes you to suffer?

Stop and Consider: How does your commute affect your relationship?

Anything that adds stress to your life also adds stress to your relationship. Could reducing your commute in some way save your relationship? Definitely. You've heard of the straw that broke the camel's back. In terms of stress, if you're near your limit, then you don't need a lot to push you over the edge. But if you can reduce your stress by doing something as mundane as reducing your commuting time, then your relationship might not have to end in disaster.

A career can have another impact on a relationship, depending on whether your work comes home with you. The most obvious impact a career can have on your home life is when the second you arrive home, you grab your smartphone and start sending work-related e-mails and texts before you even say hello to your partner. And if you're both doing it, that's not any better! Another aspect of your work-home relationship is your attitude and that of your partner. Odds are that you have a game face at the office. Maybe you have employees who report to you, or your employer counts heavily on you, so you have to steel yourself during work hours. However, going back to your true self when you arrive home can be difficult. Maybe you bark at your partner, or your partner barks at you. It might take a while for the stress that's built up during the day to decrease.

Stop and Consider: Do you bring the office home with you?

Just realizing what's taking place might be enough to overcome this particular issue, but then again, you may need to plan and make some effort to leave your work at work. You might have heard that love is strong, but it can also be fragile. You each fell in love with someone who wasn't encased in workplace armor, but now you need to realize that that armor doesn't come off that quickly and that it can have a negative impact on your relationship.

In this chapter, I've used the word "career" a lot, but many jobs aren't stepping stones to anything but a paycheck. If you or your partner is miserable at work, there's no doubt that misery will have a negative impact on your relationship. If it's just a job, then you definitely need to do all that you can to make a change regarding work. Maybe you should even take a temporary pay cut just so that you don't ruin a perfectly good relationship. Furthermore, if you don't like your job and you're bringing a dark cloud home that enshrouds your partner, start looking for a new job right away. Even if you need six months to make a switch, just knowing that there's a light at the end of the tunnel can be very helpful to your relationship. If your partner understands why you've been moping around at home, knows that he or she isn't at fault, and gets to share in basking in that light ahead, it will make the relationship that much stronger.

> **Dr. Ruth Westheimer**
> @AskDrRuth
>
> If your job is taking too strong a toll on your relationship, start looking elsewhere.

Here's a case where that 50 percent divorce rate that is bandied about can be damaging. If you look at your relationship as a disposable object, then you could easily decide that your job is more valuable than your relationship. In some cases that may be true, but I hope in most cases it's not. Your relationship should be your first priority, and you should make every effort to mitigate the damage your work life is having on your love life.

What if you're stuck in a job you hate? Maybe you have health issues and need the health insurance coverage that your job offers. Maybe other jobs with equal pay aren't available close to where you live. Maybe you're waiting for your supervisor to retire in three years so you can have that job. Whatever the reason, it's possible that leaving your job is not an option. If your job is taking its toll on your love life, then you have a big problem. The best piece of advice I can give you is to try a little harder to make the relationship work. Is it fair to be saddled with this extra burden? No, it's not, but losing your relationship in addition to having a miserable job is an even worse outcome, so try to salvage what you can.

Life isn't always fair. I certainly never wanted to become an orphan or stop growing at four foot seven. But to make the most out of life, you have to put in some extra effort to grab whatever good comes your way. Wallowing in your misery will only make it worse. And you know what? If you go out on a date with your partner even though you're tired and stressed out, I bet that you'll find the reward is worth your effort. Sometimes you have to force yourself to enjoy life.

9.

The Long-Distance Relationship

There are two primary types of long-distance relationships: those that have a fixed time period and those that are open-ended. They're both difficult to navigate, but the open-ended ones can be even tougher.

Some people—for example, couples in which one partner is in the military—go into the relationship accepting that they're going to be apart for long stretches. Such couples aren't insulated from having difficulties, but from a psychological point of view, if you've accepted a certain lifestyle to begin with, enduring the relationship is easier because there will be less second-guessing.

If the long-distance aspect is fixed, say for the number of years until graduation, knowing that at a time you can finally live in proximity to one another makes being apart easier to deal with. Both halves of the couple have something to hang on to while they tolerate their separation.

> **Dr. Ruth Westheimer**
> @AskDrRuth
>
> If a long-distance relationship has a fixed time limit, it makes being apart easier to bear.

Many long-distance relationships without a fixed time period are of the on-again, off-again variety, like the military families where the one serving goes away for long stretches of active duty, or long-distance truck drivers who are away more than they are home. At least these days, with Skype and other video-chatting apps, families have the opportunity for much better communication than in the past. But there's no doubt that these communication aids don't make up for the lack of physical closeness.

I'm writing this book for those who are considering breaking up their relationship. If you're in that situation and in a long-term, long-distance relationship, it's easy to come up with many scenarios that would lead to a breakup. Assuming there aren't children involved and the fissures between you have grown deep, my advice would be to break up sooner rather than later. It's hard enough to hold such relationships together, no less make repairs when there's been a lot of damage. If there are children, then I'd say wait until you can get back together, go for some intense therapy—meaning several visits in a week, not just one every couple of weeks—and see what happens.

Another category of long-term relationships involves couples who met on the Internet and haven't yet met in person or whose in-person meetings have been few and far between. I often say that I'm old-fashioned and a square, so maybe I'm not the person to give these individuals advice. I can understand meeting someone in person, falling in love, and then being in a long-distance relationship. Meeting someone online who lives nearby is perfectly fine; you can meet regularly if you become a couple. But falling in love with someone you barely know and who is unavailable seems reckless. It's somewhat like falling in love with a fictional character (and, of course, this online lover may be totally different than the image he or she is portraying). Remember, I value time a great deal, and because lovers need to be physically together, I would advise against giving in to such strong emotions and starting a relationship in which this close physical connection isn't possible. I'm not saying you can't fall in love this way, only that the odds of being hurt seem so high that I would caution against it. Plus, if you're spending a lot of time chatting online with this e-lover, then you're not making yourself available to find a partner who can hold you and kiss you.

Needless to say, maintaining good communication is a key factor in holding any type of long-distance relationship together. And if the fabric of that relationship is tearing, the first step you should take in making repairs is to examine the state of your communication. Both of you putting in your best efforts to stay in touch might be enough to keep the spark that brought you together alive.

Dr. Ruth Westheimer
@AskDrRuth

Long-distance relationships can thrive only if communications are in top-notch form.

Every deteriorating relationship has a tipping point, a point when the decision to stay or go becomes moot because the relationship is irreparably damaged. Being far apart can make it more difficult to understand that you've reached that point. Furthermore, making the split can be harder, because you know breaking up is better done in person, but the distance makes that impossible. As a result, a long-distance relationship can drag on, even if one of you is seriously involved with someone else, because your actions aren't visible to your partner who is many miles away.

My general theory on relationships is that you should never start a new one until the old one is officially over. This is for several reasons. The least obvious reason is that if you're miserable because of your existing relationship, someone who comes along who is only slightly better suited will look good in comparison. If after trying to make a go of it with your first partner, you break up with him or her, you can then consider this new person. You might decide that this new person is the right person for you. But after you're free of the chains of that first relationship, you might think, *I need some time to be alone* or *I can do better than this other person.* Hence, breaking off the first relationship not only is the right thing to do morally speaking but also can save you from making another mistake.

> **Dr. Ruth Westheimer**
> @AskDrRuth
>
> Starting an affair if you're in a bad relationship is a big mistake.

The temptation to cheat is a lot stronger when you're in a long-distance relationship. You're lonely and sexually frustrated, so you can easily become involved with someone who is nearby. Because the two of you involved in this long-distance relationship know you're vulnerable, one or both of you becoming jealous is another risk. And that jealousy can cause serious problems to your relationship. In fact, one of you accusing the other of cheating, even if no one is cheating, could lead that person to cheat. He or she might think, *My partner believes I'm cheating, so what have I got to lose by actually cheating?*

Stop and Consider: Is jealousy causing a rift in your long-distance relationship?

If you came to see me in my office before starting a long-distance relationship, I would advise you not to enter one, because of all the pitfalls. However, if you're already in that kind of relationship and not sure whether to stay or go, then you have a lot of self-examination to do. When you're in a relationship and you see a lot of your partner, it's easier to decide whether this person is the right one for you. I didn't say easy, just easier. But when you're far apart and you're relying a lot more on memories of what first brought you together than on what happened last night, you're in a tough situation.

For the sake of this discussion, pretend that you are in my office. My main goal is always to help the person sitting in that chair across from me. I don't try to be objective. I don't try to get my client to bend over backward to save the relationship. If my client is miserable and ending the relationship is the only way that he or she will find happiness, then that's the advice I give. If you accept that position, then it doesn't matter as much whether your partner is near or far. If you're not happy, and things aren't likely to get better within a specific period of time, then you should leave, which is especially true because long-distance relationships are so much harder to fix.

If you came to me (or some other professional) and together we succeeded in getting your partner to come to therapy with you, maybe you two could figure out a way to stay together. But if your partner is far away, that kind of guidance with both of you seeing the same therapist is unavailable. (I know technology exists that allows people to have a videoconference with a therapist, but I maintain it's not going to be as effective, though it might be better than nothing.) I'm against wasting time in a miserable relationship, and if making repairs seems unlikely, the right decision is to get out of it. The decision is right because you'll be free to find someone else and experience the happiness that will bring much sooner.

> **Dr. Ruth Westheimer**
> @AskDrRuth
>
> Sorry to report, but long-distance relationships are more vulnerable to breakups.

10.

Putting It All Together

You bought this book because you're not sure whether the relationship you're in is one to keep or end. I hope that you've learned a lot, but it's possible that you aren't any further in this decision-making process. Why hasn't my advice been sufficient? Let's put that question aside and simply accept that you're stuck, then let's figure out how to get you unstuck.

You might think that because you have only two choices, staying or going, the decision would be relatively easy. Without a doubt one choice, the decision to go, is a lot harder to make than the decision to stay or to coast (which is the same thing). Leaving is going to be heartbreaking, gut-wrenching, and just plain awful. Granted, at some point after you leave, maybe a week or so, maybe a month or so, maybe longer, you're going to feel better. But the actual process of packing your bags, and maybe moving half of the furniture from your house, is extremely difficult. And just the way your nervous system is calibrated not to touch a hot surface to avoid getting burned, your emotional system has the same aversion to being consumed by the flames of a breakup.

On the one hand, this decision-making process isn't a fair fight. Unless your relationship is in significantly bad shape, you're going to be strongly pulled into staying. And staying together could even be the right decision. But the key to making the correct choice is to make a decision, rather than leaving the course of your love life to chance. To make a decision, you have to build yourself up, train for the possibility of a breakup, and develop a game plan that will help make the exit easier. If a breakup is imminent, make sure you're prepared. The less ready you are, the less able you'll be to pull it off.

You might be thinking that because 50 percent of all marriages fail and probably a greater percentage of committed relationships don't make it, breaking up can't be that hard. Likely, though, it's that the degree of difficulty all comes down to timing. When a relationship or marriage has fallen to pieces, the decision to leave becomes a lot easier. After you've figured out that staying together is impossible, you're left with only the details of how to go about breaking up. Before you got to that point, how much pain and suffering did you go through? You want to avoid the added pain that comes during the months and maybe years of being in a relationship that should be over but instead drags on.

Stop and Consider: How long have you been thinking that perhaps your relationship isn't worth holding on to?

If you're reading this book, you know that something is wrong with your relationship, but the relationship probably isn't caustic yet. To leave, you need to shove yourself out the door, but you're not sure if doing so is the right course of action. More than likely, your relationship has occasional pain, but it likely also has occasional joy, which is what makes the decision at the pretoxic stage so difficult. (I'm not suggesting that leaving in the toxic stage is easy, just that it's inevitable, or should be.)

How do you train to make a decision about whether to stay or go? One way is to come up with other smaller decisions that are easier to make. And no, I don't mean what to have for dinner, though choosing what to eat can be tough if you're hungry and at a restaurant with a big menu. No, I'm referring to decisions having to do with your relationship. If you were learning to drive, you wouldn't start on a superhighway, would you? You'd begin on some quiet streets or maybe even in an empty parking lot. I suggest you do the same when you begin testing your relationship.

One set of decisions you can make has to do with creating a timeline. You might need to take only a casual look at your relationship to figure out certain changes that must be made for improvement (though if you dig a bit deeper, the list could grow and grow). Perhaps you've requested adjustments from your partner, but so far your partner hasn't cooperated. I suggest that you take one or two of these requests, maybe a more serious one or maybe just an annoying one, and create a deadline by when you want the change made, perhaps in a week or a month.

That deadline can come in one of two forms. The first is one you set for your partner. You can frame it something like this: "I've asked you again and again to talk to me during dinner and not watch TV. Either you stop by Monday, or I'm going to assume that you have no interest in talking to me." The other might involve the same scenario, but you're sick of asking, so rather than repeat your request, you make a promise of some change to yourself.

What could that change be? For example, say that you're normally the one who prepares dinner. As of the deadline, you prepare only your dinner. When your partner asks, "Where's my dinner?" you can say, "Because I end up eating dinner alone, I don't see the point of preparing a meal for both of us."

Making a statement like that is a challenge, but you mustn't turn it into a threat. And remember, it's not just your words that count but also your body language and your tone of voice. Try to be matter-of-fact rather than angry, if you can. As the expression goes, the ball is now in your partner's court. And your partner's reaction will likely push your relationship either into a better place or perhaps off the cliff. You have to be prepared for both possibilities. If you present it as a threat, then it's less likely that the change will be positive, because no one likes to be threatened. When faced with a fait accompli, meaning the responsibility for getting his or her own dinner, your partner will be forced to make a choice. Most importantly, your partner will know that you're serious. Without threatening to leave, you've told your partner in no uncertain terms that aspects of your relationship need to improve.

For couples therapy to be effective, both members of the couple must go. I tell people that if their partner refuses to go, they should go anyway. By going to see a therapist, you're saying in no uncertain terms that whatever you've stated is bothering you is serious. You're not going to continue to ignore it; you've decided to speak to a professional to get advice on how to proceed. More often than not, your partner will change his or her mind. That person understands that you are going to tell someone else about the issue, and he or she will want that therapist to hear both sides of the story. After speaking to each of them, the therapist should be able to arbitrate a solution.

The same effect occurs when you make the dinner challenge. Even if your partner pretends not to care and, in this case, just orders pizza, your partner will think about it and make some decisions. Your partner hopefully is going to see how important it is to you to have a conversation over dinner, decide that your love is important, and agree not to watch TV during dinner, if not right away, at least in a day or two. If your partner doesn't do the right thing, then he or she has drawn a line in the sand that you just might have to heed. Before you might have been thinking that the TV watching was just rude, but now you see that the TV means more to your partner than you do. Now you're going to look at the other aspects of your relationship and be faced with deciding whether those also show a lack of love and respect.

By having made this small decision—not to make dinner—you'll have taken an important step in making the next decision, which might be to end the relationship. By challenging yourself and your partner, you'll have changed the dynamics of the relationship, and the final outcome will become clearer.

But these "challenges" shouldn't be so upsetting that any one in and of itself causes a breakup. Remember I said that you were training yourself to make that big decision, and training takes time and effort. Winning or losing one challenge won't be enough to make you ready for that ultimate decision. And the challenge probably wouldn't be fair to your partner either. You know what the stakes are, but your partner doesn't. Going to see a therapist is a serious step, but not making dinner is much less of one. If you stick to your guns, your partner is going to know that something is up. Your partner will be forewarned that you're at least considering where the relationship is heading. You'll have sent a strong signal that change is in the air, yet you won't have laid down an ultimatum that will force a breakup.

Stop and Consider: What really bothers you about your partner and what challenge might you offer?

How many such challenges will you need to get ready? It's hard to determine the answer in advance, especially because a lot will depend on your partner's reaction. Even if your partner doesn't react to the first challenge in the way you would have wanted, your partner will know that the next challenge will likely be more significant, if for no other reason than that there will be a cumulative effect. To ignore one request might not be serious, but ignoring two or more sets a pattern. Before your partner decides whether to change his or her behavior to meet your next challenge, he or she will begin to understand the importance of these challenges. Your partner will know that you're not offering these challenges lightly and that you mean business.

Allow me to explain more about the type of challenges you should establish. Unless your partner is in the ad or news business and has to watch the evening news, the example I chose was pretty clear. Most people would agree that ignoring your partner at dinner every night is a slap in the face. (Of course, if you both are eating dinner with your faces glued to a smartphone, then this example doesn't hold up, but I've already addressed that issue earlier in this book.) Some aspects of your relationship that you don't like might be considered a personal preference. Your partner grows a beard because he doesn't like to shave, but you hate the beard because it's scratchy and he no longer looks like himself. I wouldn't consider that a good issue to challenge in this context, when you're trying to make some serious changes to your relationship. In fact, if your dislike of his beard is all you can find to address, then your relationship is going well. If your relationship is in good shape and you dislike his new beard, feel free to state your views, but because it's your partner's body and not your own, you might not get your way.

You must choose the challenge that you're issuing with care. It should be something that really bothers you and can be remedied. Remember you're not trying to cause a breakup; you're just practicing.

Think of your relationship like a large ocean liner. Big ships can't change direction on a dime. When they're in a harbor, they require tugboats to nudge them in the right direction. Your relationship is like an ocean liner, and your challenges are like those tugboats. You're not ending the relationship; you're just trying to steer it in a direction that you find more palatable, and it's going to force your partner to decide whether such changes are acceptable or not.

As it happens, you're going to have to think more carefully about your second challenge than your first. Unless your partner is dense, he or she is going to view this second challenge as part of a pattern. Your partner will see that you're testing the relationship, and his or her response will have bigger repercussions this time. Turning you down a second time will have a cumulative effect.

This could turn into a test of wills. Your partner may stand his or her ground just on the principle of not wanting to back down. This is an important piece of information to have, and it will tell you something about where you stand in this relationship. You can then start getting ready to offer a bigger challenge, one that could mean the end of the relationship.

There's also the possibility that your partner will issue a challenge of his or her own. You're probably not perfect; something about you probably bothers your partner. By taking this tack and offering a challenge in return, your partner has opened a dialogue. Everything is on the table, and now you can have some serious discussions about the state of your relationship. At that time, you should talk about going for professional therapy.

You might have been making requests like this for months and gotten nowhere, so you ask yourself, *What's different this time?* The difference is the timeline you've set. If you're going to be ignored, there are going to be consequences.

These consequences shouldn't be fights. Your partner may be good at fighting, and if you go back and look at the fights you've had, you may see that nothing of consequence ever happens, which is common in a bad relationship. By fighting back, your partner gets to feel that he or she is on equal footing with you, even though your partner's actions are undoubtedly not those of someone who loves and respects you.

And that's why I'm against ultimatums. Ultimatums—either you do this or I'll do that—lead to fights that usually don't result in making any progress in healing a relationship. Instead you ask for some change, and if your partner refuses to change, then you take direct action, as in no longer making dinner.

Here are some other examples involving a variety of issues that couples often encounter. I'm going to skip some serious ones, like catching a spouse cheating or dealing with abuse, because for most people these are signs that the relationship should end, or at least that both partners should go for serious professional counseling.

The first problem to address is boredom. To me boredom is an insidious problem that might be hard to spot but does a lot of damage. I'm not talking about sexual boredom here, although there's a connection. If you're bored in every aspect of the relationship, you're probably not going to be having great sex either. Because some people require a certain pattern to reach orgasm, sex that follows the same routine each time is sometimes the only solution. However, because most couples aren't spending a significant amount of time having sex, if the time you spend together is boring, then your relationship has a serious issue.

I often talk about how vital good communication is to holding a couple together, but if two people have nothing to talk about, then their communication is going to be minimal. As I discussed in chapter 6, having some shared interests is important. If you don't have any, you need to develop some that will have an adhesive effect on your relationship. If your partner refuses to participate in any shared activities, that won't lead to any stimulating conversation, which doesn't bode well for the relationship.

Granted, you could get a library card, bury yourself in a continuous flow of books, and keep your conversations at the grunt level. But why be in such a relationship? To share expenses? You could get a roommate for that. Love isn't something you keep in a box; it has to be expressed and passed back and forth.

The longer two people stay together, the more connections they should make and the closer they should get. What boredom does is keep those connections from being made. Instead of growing together, you actually grow apart. You start to make separate lives. Maybe he goes to play golf weekend afternoons and she goes to play cards, or they watch different TV shows in different rooms. Having separate interests is OK; you just also want to have some common interests.

Before the world became so connected, if you lived in a small rural community, your options were limited. But today if you can get online, you can explore the entire world through the Internet. If you're stuck with someone who bores you and that person won't change, then you have a problem. Start by offering a challenge or two, like suggesting a visit to a museum or watching a documentary together on a place you want to visit, and see what reaction you get.

Stop and Consider: Is your relationship boring, vibrant, or somewhere in between?

Another common problem is having a partner who works long hours; this leaves the other partner feeling alone much of the time. I'm sorry to have to put one more burden on this overworked individual, but he or she must make time for his or her partner. Always being busy and/or tired isn't acceptable. I understand financial pressures. When I first came to this country I was a single mother working as a housekeeper for a dollar an hour. The problem is if you abandon your relationship, even for a good cause such as making money, you end up damaging it. Eventually it can become so damaged that you can't repair it.

The challenges you present certainly have to be within certain bounds. Both partners are intimately familiar with their financial circumstances; however, setting aside ten minutes to discuss the day isn't too much to ask. Finding the time to make love isn't a major request. Ensuring you both make time for hugs and kisses shouldn't be an impossible ask. If it is, then maybe all the time spent at work is nothing more than an excuse not to be with one's partner. A relationship might not come before paying the rent and putting food on the table, but more than likely there's free time to allot to it.

Up to this point, I haven't mentioned the word "guilt" much, but certainly, in this example, guilt is going to play a role. If you're the partner who's feeling lonely and blue, asking for time from someone whose main fault is working so hard to bring in the money to cover your expenses may make you feel somewhat selfish and therefore somewhat guilty. But your emotional life is important. Being miserable and lonely every night isn't a way to live. If you're in a situation like this, you'll have to handle it delicately, but you also shouldn't ignore your emotional needs.

At what point might you decide that this situation is more than you can bear and you want to leave? Many factors come into play when making such a decision, so I can't give you a pat answer. Even though I might tell you to go for professional help, if you're in this situation, your finances might be too tight to afford professional counseling. Hence, I suggest that you discuss a timeline. You need to know that your relationship will one day become more emotionally satisfying. Some people are workaholics, and they don't need to work such long hours because of a financial need. They work long hours for many possible reasons; perhaps one is so they don't have to give in to their emotions and grow closer to their partner. In such instances, if you're the partner, your choices are limited to staying and being miserable or leaving. If your partner can't say something like "I need another year to build the business," then maybe you should start thinking about where you're going to be, and with whom, a year from now.

Having goals that are far apart can certainly be a reason for a breakup. Say that you want kids and your partner doesn't, or you want to live in a big city and your partner prefers a rural environment. These types of issues might not have been important when you were dating and madly in love, but when you stare into a future that has you remaining together, that's another story. You need to be sure of your own position before deciding that a situation such as one of these means that you want to end the relationship. If you're on the fence about children or where to live, then you can't expect your partner to have a change of heart.

To repeat myself, the crucial element in these types of situations is time. For example, take the question of children. If you absolutely want to have children and your partner doesn't, then your relationship is ultimately doomed. At some point, you're going to have to find someone who does want children. Don't delay one more day. Why drag the relationship out if it's ultimately doomed? Parting ways isn't going to get any easier as more time goes by. As far as issuing challenges, you have only one: "Will you change your mind about having children?" If the answer is no, then you should bite the bullet and say your goodbyes. Doing so might be sad, but in the long run it will be sadder if you miss out on the experience of having children, which another partner can offer you.

One of the issues that trips up many couples is marriage. One partner wants to get married, and the other isn't ready to commit. In such cases, you must have a good talk with yourself. The first thing to do is convince yourself that there are other people out there, plenty of them, who not only offer what your current partner does but also would agree to marry you. If that conviction isn't firmly stored in your brain, if deep down inside you're convinced that leaving this person means a life full of loneliness, then you have a problem. I'm not saying it's all you need to make the decision to leave, but it's the most vital component. You need confidence to break up with someone; you need to be in a position of strength, and if you believe that breaking up is going to ruin your life, then how can you choose that option? Only if you accept that this breakup means you'll soon be with someone else will you work up the courage to leave.

Stop and Consider: Do you truly believe that someone else is out there for you?

Nobody is perfect, and there's no such thing as soul mates. Your current partner has pros and cons, just as any future partner will (and you have them, too). If you want a partner who is willing to commit to a lifelong relationship, then you need to focus on that goal and accept that there isn't such a thing as a perfect partner.

What happens, though, when your partner says, "I love you, but I'm just not ready for marriage"? First, you have to make a list of your partner's faults. For the time being, ignore your partner's positive attributes. You want to see if there are any other possible signs that this person isn't for you, because, yes, an unwillingness to commit is a major flaw. If he or she has another major flaw, then maybe that becomes a deal breaker. Maybe you say thank you to the fates that saved you from marrying this person and move on.

If someone does say, "I love you but am not ready to commit," then a trial separation might be a good move. See how you both feel a month later. If your partner hasn't changed his or her opinion, then maybe the fact that you already have one foot out the door will prove to be a good thing. Separating is a lot easier than permanently breaking up. Permanently breaking up is also a lot easier if you're already separated.

You might have noticed that I've been careful in this book to address both men and women. From what you may hear in the media, men are more likely to avoid making a commitment. That's not entirely true with one group—older men. I've heard again and again about older men who want to commit, but they find that women drag their heels. In many instances, the woman is younger, and perhaps the age difference is one of the factors causing her to hesitate. But the men are looking for security, and they are worried about growing old without a partner.

I find this fascinating, but what does it mean for younger women who are with men who won't commit? Why are these men avoiding the security of a commitment? Although each case is slightly different, one factor influencing these men is the idea that maybe there's someone better out there for them, so they're keeping their options open. And you know what? If that's the case with your man, then I'm telling you to move on and do it ASAP. Given that marriage isn't as binding as it used to be, a partner who wants to retain his ability to play the field, to whatever degree, is one who might leave you at the first opportunity. If this partner is hesitating because of the feeling that you might not be the best person to be found, then face it, you don't want to marry this person. After you realize that, you need to start looking for someone else.

Stop and Consider: Could the reason your partner won't commit be that he or she is still hoping for someone "better" than you?

What if your partner isn't holding up his or her end regarding either traditional or contemporary roles? For example, either he insists on always splitting the tab, or he won't allow you to ever pay your share. I know this may not be PC, but I don't always agree when it comes to following a certain set of arbitrary "rules." Maybe you could say I'm being inconsistent, but I want a man who will both give me the freedom that I need *and* hold the door for me. Given my position, I give legitimacy to any expectations you have for a partner. If your partner is a man who is indecisive and lets you call all the shots, or if your partner is a woman who doesn't dress in a feminine manner, he or she might not be someone you want to spend the rest of your life with. Don't let society influence you into accepting someone whose views don't match yours or fulfill your needs. If two people want to switch traditional roles and she wears the pants, that's fine. Or if they don't want to have any roles and just build their relationship one piece at a time, that's fine, too. But if, for example, you're a woman who wants a man who holds the door for you and yours won't, then you're entitled to move on.

You might have noticed this characteristic when you first met, or perhaps you've only realized it recently, but either way you have a right to your opinion. Of course, so does your partner. The question, though, is whether your partner understands how much of a problem this flaw is for you. Bringing it up after six months of dating or even several years of marriage is going to seem weird. "What took you so long?" is likely to be a retort, not to mention, "Either take me as I am or . . ."

People don't change their personalities all that readily, and nobody is perfect. So you need to have this discussion with yourself. Can you live with your partner's quirks given everything else you like about this person, or if you peer into your crystal ball, are these quirks going to bother you more and more?

Stop and Consider: Do you really want to make a lifetime commitment to your partner?

A person can have many flaws, some of which are personal to you, such as not being a traditionalist when that's what you prefer, and some of which would be problems for anyone. Some people can't seem to always tell the truth. Some have a huge ego that constantly needs to be stroked. Others are drama queens who turn everything into a huge production. Your partner's ties to his or her family may be so strong that they're damaging your relationship. Your partner may have some psychological issues, such as depression, that make life together less fun. Someone who is extremely sensitive and touchy, which makes you feel like you're always stepping on eggshells, can make being together uncomfortable.

Stop and Consider: What are your partner's faults, both the major ones and the minor ones?

Nobody is perfect, and you bring your share of imperfections to the relationship as well. The problem with the flaws that you identified in your partner is that they're not necessarily of the make-or-break variety, which leaves you undecided about your dilemma. This flawed partner of yours undoubtedly has some pluses to go with the minuses. After all, you did fall in love with him or her, and love can override a flaw or two. Or can it?

So here you are at the toughest question: Do the pluses in your relationship outweigh the minuses? If so, by how much? If it's a 50/50 split, I'd tell you to head for the door. Why? The odds are that the relationship isn't going to improve. Every relationship occasionally hits rough spots, and if your relationship is hanging in the balance, then at some point it won't survive something problematic that life throws your way. Given that situation, and combined with my philosophy about wasting time, your decision is simple: leave to find someone else whose positive qualities far outweigh his or her negative ones. As I see it, 50/50 equals goodbye. But what if it's 55/45 or 60/40? And can you even measure such differences?

The answer is the difference probably can't be measured if it's close to 50/50. If you've been trying, then you've only been wasting your time. If you've spent hours and hours playing "Should I stay or should I go?" in your head, then you need a new game plan. Your decision can't be based on anything external, like your partner's great smile or nail-biting habit. At least in your head, when you add the good and the bad, you get a number that doesn't lead to a decision, which is a big mistake when it comes to a relationship. You must decide whether you want to remain in the relationship or get out, if for no other reason than to maintain your own sanity. If you don't reach a decision, the same thoughts about what attracts you and what makes you cringe about your partner will keep running through your head and drive you crazy. If you decide to stay, then you can teach yourself to overlook your partner's faults. But if you're just drifting along in the relationship, then those faults are going to haunt you for as long as you're together. So what you need to do is adopt a philosophy.

I've told you mine several times in this book, but let me repeat it here: people are given far too little time on this earth, and life is too precious to waste; therefore, when judging a relationship, if it isn't one that is clearly worth being in, you should get out of it.

I developed my philosophy from my life experiences. Because I lost my family and almost died on several occasions, I developed the belief that I need to fill my days with as much happiness as I can for myself, and in honor of my departed family members. It's wrong to wallow in misery, so instead I move on. And if this philosophy causes me to make a mistake, I accept it, which is an important point. You might decide on an entirely different philosophy. You might just cast your fate to the wind and, rather than make decisions, wait to see what happens next. That philosophy is fine, as long as you accept what happens. But if you're stewing in a relationship that isn't bringing you the joy you imagined, then you're not following your own philosophy. You're not being carefree and accepting of your life; you're just allowing yourself to be miserable.

Stop and Consider: Is your level of happiness or unhappiness under your control?

Some people have as a philosophy that when faced with a problem, they're going to keep working at it until it becomes better. Based on that philosophy, if the relationship has problems, people just keep hammering away at them, which is fine as long as they like this sort of challenge and they're not constantly complaining about their relationship.

Some have adopted the role of martyr. They pretty much expect that things will go wrong, so when something does, rather than try to fix it, they look at it as their fate. This philosophy may not stop them from feeling badly about a relationship that's not going well, but instead of wasting a lot of time worrying about it, they will just accept it.

Others are extremely religious and turn to prayer. Although I go to temple fairly regularly and pray, when it comes to something like a bad relationship, I don't trouble God. I just take the necessary steps to walk away. If people want to leave their fate in God's hands, that's their business, but apart from praying for a better life, they need to stop complaining about their lot.

Others turn to research, mostly on the Internet. They read as much as they can about relationships, looking for examples that resemble what they're going through and searching for an answer. If you go that route, you have to set a limit on how much research you're going to do. The odds are that the solution isn't online, but rather inside your own brain. It's a decision that you need to make, and you probably have more information than you need already. If doing this research makes you feel better, and if your relationship problems aren't severe, then this approach might work for you. I shouldn't complain, because it's probably why you bought this book. But you can only go so far in analyzing a relationship by doing research. Your feelings have a lot to do with your final decision, and they're located inside you, not in a computer. Learning how to analyze what you're feeling is OK, but you can only go so far alone. At some point, you may need professional guidance, which is something I recommend highly.

11.

How to Leave

If you've decided to leave your current relationship, your next step is to figure out exactly how you're going to proceed. If you don't live together, then accomplishing the breakup can be easier; however, if you share space, an acrimonious parting is a recipe for extra pain.

If you're leaving because your partner is verbally or physically abusive or has cheated—in other words, you have irrefutable reasons and leaving will cause you little remorse—you don't have to make it all that complicated. You do have to prepare carefully. You want to be the one who is doing the blindsiding and not the other way around.

If your financial affairs are in any way intertwined or if you've signed any documents together, such as a lease, then consult with an attorney. Why? You may be able to get this soon-to-be ex-partner to agree to certain things if you're still on good terms, but after you've said goodbye, if your partner feels that you've been unfair and wants to take revenge, then you'll be more vulnerable. An attorney can guide you through this minefield and help you to come out with the least amount of damage.

Stop and Consider: After you part, is there anything you'll still be legally or financially responsible for?

An important question can be timing. If you leave without any sort of agreement, you could be giving up rights. Sometimes it's better to stick it out for a little while longer to save yourself a lot of grief in later battles. Remember, in this case I'm speaking to readers who are married or living together; their lives are more intermingled than people who are in a relationship but don't live together.

Might your split be of the "let's stay friends" variety? It could be, but are you sure that's what is going to happen? Splitting up is very painful—not just for you but also for your partner. People react differently when under that type of stress, so I suggest you prepare for the worst-case scenario while hoping for the best.

Stop and Consider: How is your partner likely to react when getting this news?

When you tell your partner you're leaving, you may also have the desire to get some things off your chest. If you're the one who's making the first move, you're speaking volumes by taking that step. You also don't have to justify yourself. Will venting your feelings make you feel better? Perhaps, but it may also lead to one last fight that will make you feel worse. Take satisfaction in being the decision-maker, and don't stretch the process out any longer than necessary.

From a psychological perspective, the most important mental tool you have is your resolve. Appearing to waver when you make your big announcement will change the entire tenor of the conversation. Your partner will sense an opening to try to win you back, which will make closure difficult. And closure is important because you don't want to be deluged with texts, e-mails, and voice mails from your partner asking you to let him or her back into your life. Maybe you can't stop those plaintive missives from being sent, but at least you have to try. Do everything you can to make the point that the relationship is over. To do so successfully, you have to believe it 100 percent, and you have to convince your partner of your belief. If you leave any wiggle room, you'll regret it. The time for wiggle room is before you say goodbye. Give this important person in your life every opportunity to make the relationship work. You owe that to both of you. But you also can't allow the process to continue forever. So after you've set a deadline, you must stick to it.

> **Dr. Ruth Westheimer**
> @AskDrRuth
>
> Goodbyes have to be final. Wiggle room is no longer welcome.

Now I'm going to contradict myself a bit, but humans are complex, so one size doesn't fit all. More than likely you've been annoyed by labor strikes of one sort or another. You say to yourself, they're going to settle it eventually, so why do they have to bother the rest of us by striking? The answer is that brinksmanship is a part of human nature. At times, everyone needs to be pushed to the edge to make a compromise. When a couple separate, the partner who wouldn't compromise might take a second look at the situation and make a counteroffer. Then you must decide whether you want to enter a new phase of negotiations, which means answering some questions.

The first of these questions is, is this an honest offer? When an offer is made under duress (and saying that you're going to leave is a form of duress), then your partner might be crossing his or her fingers behind his or her back. The offer might not be a serious one, at least not in the long run. Because you've been lovers and know this person well, you can make that judgment call. If your now ex is someone you can't trust, then you keep on walking. But if you feel this compromise is one that he or she will live up to, then you have a decision to make.

Another vital question is, do you really want back into this relationship? Maybe making this decision to leave lifted a great weight off your shoulders. Maybe you can't wait to go off on your own. You might feel badly rejecting the offer being made in response to your revelation, but, in the end, you know it's the correct decision. In that case, you just have to stick to your guns. If you want to put an end to the discussion, and assuming you have your exit strategy planned, ask for some time to think about it, even if you know you're not going to change your mind.

Stop and Consider: Are you 100 percent sure you want to leave?

On the other hand, if you were secretly hoping that saying you were leaving was going to get your partner to beg you to stay, then fine, latch onto the offer. If later you realize that your initial decision to leave was the correct one, then you can still carry out that plan. At least after giving the relationship a second chance, you'll have more confidence in leaving the next time, if you do.

No matter how good an offer your partner makes, a better one might come your way if you hold out a little longer, so don't automatically leap back into your partner's arms. Whatever your grievances were, they were legitimate. They weren't so minor that your partner is going to be able to completely turn things around. Some behaviors are ingrained and can be cast aside only with a lot of effort. Really, neither of you know whether your relationship can be repaired. Take your time, protecting your heart a little in case in a matter of weeks, days, or even hours, you realize that your decision to leave was the right one.

There's also the possibility that your partner made his or her offer in desperation. If your announcement to leave was unexpected, the immediate thought of losing you may have seemed so terrible that your partner was willing to make any concession. If the thought of breaking up hadn't occurred to your partner yet, bringing it up might be the spark needed to convince your partner that separation is the best choice. Even if you do get back together, don't be entirely surprised if suddenly the shoe is on the other foot, and your partner says his or her goodbye.

Have I confused you by telling you to stick to your guns and telling you it's OK to let this person back into your life? If you were in my office and I really knew all the details of the relationship, I wouldn't be so wishy-washy, but I don't know anything about your relationship, and to set down hard-and-fast rules would be foolish. If you're really confused—not because of my advice but because of the complexities of your relationship—then go get some help. Professional advice would be best, but if you don't have the means to get that, find an older relative you trust or a religious leader.

What about a friend? You're going to need your friends in your new single life to lift your spirits and take you away from the pain of the breakup. If one or more friends are intimately involved in the breakup, then seeing them will only remind you of what you just went through, so to the extent that you can keep them out of the process, the better.

And what if you confide your problems to a friend who ends up giving you the wrong advice? You'd be right to be angry, and you might lose that friend as well as your partner. Ask your friends to help you through this breakup by being supportive, not by being your analyst. In the end, you'll be better served.

So, returning to the subject at hand, how do you leave? You should talk in person unless you're in a long-distance relationship, or unless your partner is abusive and might get violent. In the latter case, you have my blessings to sneak away in the dead of night never to be heard from again. Otherwise, don't leave in an impersonal manner just because doing it in person is hard. Experience has probably taught you that the more difficult something is to do, the bigger the rewards. The reward in this situation is a lessening of guilt. You might feel guilty no matter what, but if you leave without really saying goodbye, then your guilt will be greater.

Another reason to tell your about-to-be ex in person is that if you don't, he or she is going to tell everyone he or she knows that you did your dumping via text / e-mail / voice mail / a note taped to the mirror / Facebook defriending, which makes you look bad. Why should you care what his friends and family think of you? The problem with you looking bad is that it makes your ex look good. No matter how rotten a person he or she might be, if the way you leave can be interpreted as rude and boorish, you end up wearing the black hat. And for what? To save yourself one last unpleasant encounter or bitter argument? Your reputation is worth more.

This conversation doesn't have to last for hours, though both of you may be tempted to drag out this parting. When communicating in person, you have no choice but to hear your partner out, but you don't have to respond. If you've made up your mind, then also make sure that you don't get sucked into a drawn-out fight. By this time, you've told your partner what displeases you about the relationship, so all you're doing is giving the relationship its final ending. If your partner had no idea that a breakup was on the horizon, then I must say that you're somewhat at fault. If you've spent years together, haven't complained, and suddenly leave, that situation would leave anyone upset and confused. Some people don't get subtle hints, and if that's your partner, then you had a duty to be more than subtle.

Enough dwelling on the exceptions. In all likelihood, whatever is wrong with the relationship is something you've both known about for quite some time. You may not agree on who is most at fault or what was needed to fix it, but the odds are that this moment isn't coming as a complete surprise. That doesn't mean it will be easy, though there are couples who part as friends, which is not a bad goal to have. How you take your leave will have a role to play in how you end up feeling about each other.

Being able to part as friends will depend on why you aren't able to remain a couple. Is the need to break up one-sided, or have you both changed your minds about each other? If you've both moved on, then a friendly parting of the ways is more likely. If only one of you is dissatisfied, then trying to keep the breakup as simple as possible will be your goal, rather than leaving a few roots that you'll always both share.

If you and your partner have children, then you'll have no choice but to remain in contact. Keeping your relationship as civil as possible is important, if not for you, then for the children.

Regardless of whether you want to stay friends, surprise shouldn't be one of your goals. Because this breakup will create a major change in your partner's life, you want the announcement of the end to be as smooth as possible and to make sure that your partner has an idea of what is going to happen. Remember I'm against making threats, but that doesn't mean you can't leave clues. You might phrase them in the following ways to put the onus on your partner: "I guess you really don't want to stay together, do you?" Or "I don't recognize the person I met a year ago." Or "Is that how you express your love for me?" If you do this too often, when you really want to announce that you're going out the door for good, you might not be believed. Hence, you need to be judicious about using these phrases. If there's something your partner does that really irks you, then use one of these phrases, but not every time things aren't going right.

I admit that I'm an impatient person. So when I reach my breaking point, I want to be able to use my favorite word: "done." Yet here I'm telling you to stretch out the process. My reason: you and your partner once loved each other, and maybe you still do to some extent. You've made the decision to end the relationship, so you owe it to your past love to make this parting a little less painful. By building up to this announcement, you'll be building up your own resolve. Each time your partner does something to annoy you, and you drop a hint that this might be the last time you permit this, you'll be more convinced of your decision, because as you begin this process you're probably going to have some doubt. If you're planning to leave and you lay out the groundwork, you'll see that when you finally say, "That's it," you'll feel better about it. You're going to feel miserable, even if you hate your partner. You're going to have to mourn the love that died. Breaking up isn't going to be easy, so the better prepared you are, the better you'll feel in that moment when you say it's over.

And be forewarned: the more you loved each other, the deeper the hurt will be. At one point the relationship had the potential for something lasting, so now that you're admitting that your love has gone up in smoke, you're going to regret what might have been. The better things were at the beginning, the more you'll feel you lost and the more painful it will be. But this also means that you're capable of a deep love, and you'll find somebody else. You must hold on to the faith that a partner is out there.

Remember, don't try to stifle your emotions. It's hard to do, but the only way to prevent one emotion from overpowering you is to cut yourself off from all your emotions, not just the sadness that you feel. If you're successful, it can be hard to turn those emotions back on again. Imagine a life of never laughing or enjoying or loving or yes, crying. You don't want to overdo your mourning, but you don't want to avoid it either.

What should you say exactly? I'm not a scriptwriter, and you're not living in a movie. You can rehearse what you're going to say over and over, but your partner is also involved in this conversation. After you've uttered your first sentence, you can't predict how the rest of the conversation will go.

The most important piece of advice I can give you is to listen. After you've said that you're leaving, your partner probably won't hear much beyond the sound of his or her blood rushing in his or her head, certainly not the words coming out of your mouth. Even if you stop him or her from talking by saying something like "First listen to what I have to say," a flood of thoughts will ensure that your partner will find it impossible to really pay attention to you. Rather than trying to explain yourself, just listen to what your partner says. If he or she asks you direct questions, maybe your answers will get through. However, if you want to start off with a soliloquy, your audience won't be paying attention.

Any other time the two of you had a serious discussion or fight, getting your point across was important. You were trying to convince your partner that you were in the right; however, during this conversation, right and wrong are off the table. The only thing you need to communicate is goodbye. And for that, short and sweet is best, at least for your mental health. Your partner may try to hold on to the past, but at this point you're looking only to the future, and a future without this partner.

What if you're in a long-distance relationship? The fact that you can't break up in person will make the discussion both harder and easier. The harder part will fall mostly on your partner. He or she will probably feel that if he or she could have spent more time with you, the breakup wouldn't have occurred, and now, he or she is unable to prevent it because it's not happening in person. This will make it easier on you, depending on the method of breakup you choose—in writing or via phone or video call—to end the discussion. But you might also feel a lot more guilt ending the relationship from afar, so that might balance out the "easy" part.

One advantage of breaking up via a letter or e-mail is that you can spend some time writing it out so that you can completely express the thought process that went into making this decision. What I said earlier about your partner not really listening to you won't apply. In fact, your partner will probably read what you wrote several times before even trying to communicate back. And because you're not saying goodbye in person, you do owe your partner a more detailed explanation. You don't want your communication to be perceived as the easy way out. You don't want your partner to be able to say, "Why didn't you wait until we could be together?" By going into detail, you can make the point that the end was inevitable whether you were face-to-face or not.

As you cut yourself off from this past with your now ex-partner, the next question is, how soon after the breakup should you start dating? I know, I know, you're saying, "Dr. Ruth, it's too early to be thinking about that." But knowing when to start dating again is the key to starting this new phase of your life. You're moving on to find someone who will love you the way you want to be loved. For your mental health, say to yourself, "I'm no longer part of a couple, but I don't want to spend the rest of my life single." You're certainly not going to hit the dating scene on the day you say goodbye, but don't automatically push away the idea of dating. For those who've decided that the single life is the better path, look closely at that decision to see how much it was colored by a bad relationship. My guess is that after a while, you'll start to miss the benefits that a loving relationship—which you weren't having at the end—offers.

When you start to date is an individual decision, but I'd say you should begin sooner rather than later for several reasons. A long delay will make it more difficult to start dating again. You could turn the question of when into a momentous decision, but it doesn't need to be. The more pressure you put on this new phase of your life, the more tension a first date will have. If you jump back into the dating pool fairly quickly, that first date won't have as much pressure on it. Also, the sooner you start dating, the easier it will be to push out those feelings of being lonely and of missing your ex. You'll shift from looking backward to looking forward. You'll stop replaying the awful moments of your last relationship and instead have pleasant fantasies about your future.

However, after you start dating again, stay away from revenge dating, where you hope that word gets back to your ex that you're not sitting at home moping. That could lead you right into a new set of problems. Remember that one of the reasons you left was to be able to start over and find happiness, so the sooner you start down that road, the easier it will be to forget the time you wasted. Let everyone know that you're open to meeting new people, but also keep your guard up so that when your heart leaps it will be into the arms of someone who really cares for you.

Can it ever be too soon to start a new relationship? It depends on your motive and the other person. Perhaps you've been miserable for a long stretch, which could make you vulnerable to the wrong kind of relationship. But if you meet someone who feels right, then you also shouldn't not date him or her just because you haven't known each other for that long. To make this decision, you have to know yourself. If you're feeling weak, then don't get serious with anyone. If you're feeling strong, then be careful, but don't be too cautious either.

12.

You Still Can't Make Up Your Mind

You've thought about all my advice and considered your current situation, yet you're no closer to your decision to stay or go than you were before you even opened this book.

Children want to become adults in part so that they can make the decisions instead of their parents deciding for them. After you become an adult, you discover that making decisions isn't as easy as it looks. Making decisions is almost never a choice between black and white, but rather between several shades of gray. (And yes, I did read all three books. See, I can read your mind!)

One reason that you're stuck is that this decision is serious, so you don't want to make a mistake. You don't want to make a decision that you'll regret later.

People come to me looking for advice, and when they're in my office I don't hesitate to give it to them. But bear in mind that I'm a behavioral therapist, not a psychologist or psychiatrist. Rather than doing analysis, I try to help people improve their lives by getting them to act in a certain way. If a couple come to me and the woman is having difficulties reaching orgasm, I give both partners homework assignments that usually solve their problem. So what homework would I give to you, a person stuck between that proverbial rock and hard place?

First, you need to do something and take some form of action to move matters along. Start small. What small change in behavior or what favor could you ask of your partner? This favor would have to relate to one of the problems the two of you are experiencing. So, for example, say that one relationship problem you are having is that he never wants to have dinner at your parents'. He doesn't want to have dinner at his parents' either, but that doesn't bother you so much. However, going to eat dinner at your parents' without ever bringing him embarrasses you, especially given all the questions you're asked each and every time. As a result, you come up with a compromise. You want him to go out to dinner with your parents at a restaurant—at a neutral location—so he shouldn't feel so threatened or whatever it is he feels about going to their home. And you've made up your mind that if he refuses, you're going to leave the relationship. That refusal is going to tip the scales from gray to black. You choose the challenge here, and you can make it as small or large as you want, but no matter what it is, you'll know its decisive nature. (And maybe the question you choose to make your stand—one you know how your partner will respond to—will show you that deep down you've already made up your mind, and this test is only to prove yourself correct.)

What's the point of doing this? You're finding this decision impossibly hard to make. So you need a gimmick. You need a flip of a coin, but it can't be the actual flip of a coin, because my guess is that you won't obey it. You'll be like the young man playing she loves me, she loves me not with flower petals; he'll keep picking new flowers until he gets the answer he wants. Although this challenge is like a coin flip, it's also more than a coin flip, because whether the coin comes up heads or tails isn't up to you but to your partner. And it's a one-shot deal.

If your partner goes to the dinner and behaves himself, then at the very least you have some more leeway to see if you can make additional refinements. Maybe looking for major improvements rather than baby steps was a mistake you were making. If he refuses, then make your escape plan. And stick to it.

And stop making excuses! Yes, excuses are often what stop people from making a decision or taking action. They range from timing (it's almost his birthday, our anniversary, Valentine's Day) to outside events (I've got this big project at work coming up, and I need to have my head together) to just plain fear of the unknown.

Your friends can play a helpful role here. You've made your decision to leave, but you're still hesitating. In that situation, tell your friends that you're leaving. Don't ask them for their opinion; just inform them. Most will support you and help push you. They might even have solutions to offer for any practical considerations ("You can sleep on my couch for as long as you need to!").

Are you one of those people who make New Year's resolutions every year, and by January 15 they've turned to dust? The better way to handle such resolutions is to make one a month and not a dozen on December 31. The same rule applies when resolving to leave.

If you have a laundry list of items to accomplish to prepare yourself for leaving, including telling your partner what you're about to do, you're more likely to put the entire list aside. I suggest that you divide and conquer. For instance, say one of the items on your list is looking for a new place to stay. Finding and renting a new apartment is a time-consuming and costly step, and it can easily become an excuse. But if your parents live nearby and would gladly take you back to get you out of the clutches of your partner, then let them know that you're coming.

Make your list and number it—not in order of importance, as telling your partner would be number one—but in order of what you need to do first. As you do each item, check it off the list. Open your own bank account, check. Copy any important documents off the computer, check. Taking care of these items might take a little while, but you'll see that as you check off more and more, reaching the final goal will seem easier, because you'll be properly prepared. As your confidence rises, you'll discover that finally informing your partner of your decision will be easier.

I've contradicted myself a few times in this book, and let me do it again. I've said that you should tell your partner that you're leaving in person, and I still think that's true. But what if you're one of those people who just can't do it? What if that particular aspect of the whole leaving thing is what's stopping you? Does it make sense to stay together just because you can't gather up the courage to confront your partner? The answer is no. If you need to leave, you need to leave, and that takes precedence. Pack your bags, and write a well-thought-out letter that will relieve your guilty conscience somewhat.

Some women insist that when giving birth they absolutely don't want an epidural, while others take the position that as soon as they start feeling too much pain, they want the injection. Neither approach is wrong. The goal is to give birth to the baby, and it's the same with leaving a relationship. You have to figure out what works for you. If leaving is the right thing to do, then doing that is most important. If the primary obstacle is having that awful conversation, then don't have it.

And if it makes you feel better, leave a bottle of his or her favorite scotch or vodka. Does that sound weird? Remember, I'm a behavioral therapist. I try to help people to take action, not just talk about their problems. And sometimes you have to trick yourself into doing the right thing. If leaving makes you feel extremely guilty, then find ways of alleviating that guilt. The act of leaving is a strong statement, so you don't have to worry about what messages you might be sending by leaving a parting gift. The gift (or whatever mental trick you might end up using) isn't really for your now ex; it's for you, because it helps you say goodbye.

Another mental trick you can you use to get over this fear-of-leaving hump is to tell your lover that you're going on vacation with some friends or a relative, that you're going on a business trip, or that an out-of-town relative has an "emergency" that you need to help with. Any trip like this will give you the excuse to pack a bag with everything important, and it will give you a week or so to get yourself settled elsewhere.

I recognize that this would be a lie, but as I've stated, I'm in favor of white lies. True, this is more than a white lie, but if an escape hatch is needed, then, as they say, all is fair in love and war.

If leaving was difficult for you, make the break as clean as possible. Tell the post office to forward your mail somewhere else so you don't have to go over to your former residence to pick it up. If you went to a religious service together, find a new place to worship so you don't run into your ex. Look for all the ways your lives have been intersecting, and cut each of those branches off. After a while you'll be less vulnerable. However, in the beginning you don't need reminders of the past, just paths toward your future.

Final Thoughts

One of my least favorite words is "normal." I'm always getting questions such as "What is the normal frequency with which a couple should have sex per week?" My reaction to such questions is "Who cares?" If the normal age of death is eighty-two, are you going to jump in front of a bus when you hit age eighty-three? You might want more or less sex from your partner (a desire that usually prompts such questions), but that request has nothing whatsoever to do with what everybody else is doing. The frequency with which you have sex is something only the two of you can determine.

The statistic that 50 percent of all marriages end in divorce resembles the word "normal" in that it influences people. But it shouldn't. When deciding whether to stay or go, all that should influence you is your perspective on the state of your relationship, not how many other couples are breaking up at that moment. Is the relationship a good one or a bad one? How good and how bad? The answers to such questions are subjective. Only you can make that decision. Leaving a relationship that someone else might think is fine or staying in one that everyone else thinks is terrible is perfectly OK. It's how *you* feel about it that counts.

Stop and Consider: Is your opinion of the state of your relationship based on how you feel, or are outside influences affecting your perspective?

Separating your feelings about your relationship from the influence that others—family, friends, society in general—have on those feelings isn't always easy. It will probably take some effort to free yourself from those opinions. How successful you are may depend on how much the opinions of others tend to influence you in general. Do you buy certain brands because you like them or because you've been influenced by those around you (or by advertising)? Do you attend a certain church, vote for a particular party, or follow one team based only on how you feel, or have your feelings been influenced by how you've been raised? Would you have a relationship with someone of a different race, religion, or culture, knowing the flack that you might get? It's easy for me to tell you to filter out those influences, but if you don't like fighting the current, then maybe you need to weigh those influences. Remember that in the end, it's all about how you feel. If outside influences make you feel badly about your relationship, then you need to consider them. Maybe they aren't a deciding factor, but they're a factor nevertheless.

People often get hung up when making the stay-or-go decision when the relationship is sending them mixed messages. A terrible day makes you want to leave, but then several good days follow, so you're not so sure. In these cases, instead of looking at individual instances, as I said in earlier chapters, you have to study the overall pattern. No relationship is perfect; every relationship has good days and bad days, so ask whether the good days, in general, outweigh the bad ones. That question can be turned into a simple math problem. Keep a daily diary of your relationship, and rate each day as mostly good, mostly bad, or in the middle. At the end of the month, add up each column. If the bad days are outnumbering the good days, then you have something to think about.

Don't think about all this too much. In other words, don't drive yourself crazy. If you've read this book, stopped, and thought when I asked you to, and you still don't have a clear answer of what to do, then for a while, put aside the whole idea of leaving. I'm sure you've heard that some couples who are struggling to have a baby end up getting pregnant when they stop trying. Being tense about a particular difficulty you're facing ends up making it harder to overcome. Clearly for some of you making this decision is very hard. So if you're in that category, my advice is to just stop thinking about it for at least a month. Ignore the things that bother you about your partner. Go about your daily life, and when the stay-or-go decision crops up, push it aside. To accomplish this, you may have to tell yourself that you've decided to stay. Don't worry about it; you can change your mind later. If you can make yourself a little more dispassionate about the subject, then maybe your brain will be able to come up with the right decision a month later when you revisit the question.

The other item on your to-do list during this month is to try to get the rest of your life in order, or at least in a better place. If you have an assortment of difficulties, they are going to have a negative impact on how you view your relationship. For example, if you're always grumpy, then your partner will have a harder time winning your favor. I understand that you can't straighten your entire life out in a month, but just making some progress will change your attitude about your relationship. If your life is on an upward swing, even a little, you'll look at your relationship differently.

Many psychologists and therapists just ask questions. They won't tell you what to do; instead, they'll say you have to decide. I'm not like that. If I think a client is making a mistake, I tell him or her. If you were in my office and after hearing your story, I thought you should leave your current relationship, you'd hear me say that in no uncertain terms. Of course, you're not in my office, so I don't know your entire story. But I do know, from the fact that you've read this book, that your relationship has issues. And although I can't tell you what to do, I can tell you how to do it, and the answer is make your final assessment and then take action. What you don't want is to remain in the stay-or-go limbo.

Deciding to stay doesn't mean that your life will suddenly be a bed of roses. Whatever issues you had will remain. You've just decided that they're not overwhelming enough to cause a breakup. Having made that decision, you must instigate a plan of action to make sure that you don't approach this same decision point again. You must take preventative measures rather than just sit around and wait for the next crisis.

An advantage of having reached a crisis point once is that it should force you to realize that you can't take anything for granted. You can't take your relationship for granted or assume that you'll be together forever, and most importantly, you can't take each other for granted, which is why you must inform your partner of your decision to stay. If you had decided to end the relationship, your partner would soon have found out about this decision. But because you've decided to stay, you potentially could have reached this crisis point without telling your partner how close you were to saying goodbye. I'm telling you not to do that. Your partner must understand that your relationship came close to ending and that you each need to take responsibility for its future. Even though I'm delighted that you looked to me for consultation, I don't want you to have to pick up this book again in six months because you're back at that same stay-or-go decision point.

ACKNOWLEDGMENTS

Dr. Ruth K. Westheimer's Acknowledgments

To the memory of my entire family who perished during the Holocaust. To the memory of my late husband, Fred, who encouraged me in all my endeavors. To my current family: my daughter, Miriam Westheimer, EdD; son-in-law Joel Einleger, MBA; their children, Ari and Leora; my son, Joel Westheimer, PhD; daughter-in-law Barbara Leckie, PhD; and their children, Michal and Benjamin. I have the best grandchildren in the entire world!

Thanks to all the many family members and friends for adding so much to my life. I'd need an entire chapter to list them all, but some must be mentioned here: Pierre Lehu and I have now collaborated on two dozen books; he's the best minister of communications I could have asked for! Cliff Rubin, my assistant, thanks! Dr. Peter Banks; Simon and Stefany Bergson; Nate Berkus; Michael Berra; David Best, MD; Frank Chervenak, MD; Richard Cohen, MD; Martin Englisher; Cynthia Fuchs Epstein, PhD; Howard Epstein; Raul Galoppe, PhD; Meyer Glaser, PhD; David Goslin, PhD; Amos Grunebaum, MD; Herman Hochberg; David Hryck, Esq.; Steve Kaplan, PhD; Rabbi Barry Dov Katz and Shoshi Katz; Bonnie Kaye; Patti Kenner; Robert Krasner, MD;

Nathan Kravetz, PhD; Marga Kunreuther; Dean Stephen Lassonde; Matthew and Vivian Lazar; Rabbi and Mrs. William Lebeau; Robin and Rosemary Leckie; Hope Jensen Leichter, PhD; Jeff and Nancy Jane Loewy; John and Ginger Lollos; Sanford Lopater, PhD, and Susan Lopater; Rafael Marmor; David Marwell; Marga Miller; Peter Niculescu; Dale Ordes; Rabbi James and Elana Ponet; Leslie Rahl; Bob and Yvette Rose; Debra Jo Rupp; Larry and Camille Ruvo; Simeon and Rose Schreiber; Daniel Schwartz; Amir Shaviv; David Simon, MD; Betsy Sledge; William Sledge, MD; Mark St. Germain; Henry and Sherri Stein; Jeff Tabak, Esq., and Marilyn Tabak; Malcolm Thomson; Ryan White; Greg Willenborg and Ilse Wyler-Weil. And to all the people at Amazon Publishing who worked so hard to bring this book into the world: Jeff Belle, Erin Calligan Mooney, Chad Sievers, and the entire team, as well as Amazon's founder and his wife who, by inviting me to Campfire, launched this endeavor, Jeff and MacKenzie Bezos.

Pierre A. Lehu's Acknowledgments

Thanks to my wife, Joanne Seminara; my son, Peter; my daughter-in-law, Melissa Sullivan; my fantastic grandsons, Jude Sullivan Lehu and Rhys Sullivan Lehu; my daughter, Gabrielle; my son-in-law, Jim Frawley, and their adorable daughter, Isabelle. And of course, to Dr. Ruth K. Westheimer for allowing me the privilege of working on so many of her books.

ABOUT THE AUTHORS

Dr. Ruth K. Westheimer is a psychosexual therapist who sprang to national attention in the early 1980s with her live radio program, *Sexually Speaking*. She went on to have her own TV program, appeared on the cover of *People* magazine and *TV Guide*, and is the author of thirty-seven books. Fans of all ages can find her at www.drruth.com, on Twitter under the handle @AskDrRuth, and at www.youtube.com/drruth. A one-woman show about her life, *Dr. Ruth, All the Way*, is currently touring. Dr. Ruth teaches at Teachers College, Columbia University. She lives in New York and has two children and four grandchildren.

Pierre A. Lehu is a publicist, agent, and writer. He has written twenty-five books, including *Sex for Dummies* with Dr. Ruth, *Saké: Water from Heaven*, *Fashion for Dummies* with Jill Martin, and *Living on Your Own: The Complete Guide to Setting Up Your Money, Your Space, and Your Life*.